ECHELON

'... with the batteries vomiting forth upon us shells and shot, round and grape, with one battery on our right flank and another on the left ... when we came to within a distance of fifty yards from the mouths of the artillery which had been hurling destruction upon us, we were, in fact, surrounded and encircled by a blaze of fire.'

Lord Cardigan

ECHELON

The Light Brigade Action at Balaclava

A NEW PERSPECTIVE

JAMES W. BANCROFT

SPELLMOUNT

*This book is dedicated to my
grandchildren.*

*We must not forget those who have gone
before us and prepared the path on which
we walk.*

First published 2011 by Spellmount, an imprint of
The History Press
The Mill, Brimscombe Port
Stroud, Gloucestershire, GL5 2QG
www.thehistorypress.co.uk

British Library Cataloguing in Publication Data.
A catalogue record for this book is available from the British
Library.

ISBN 978 0 7524 6207 3

Typesetting and origination by The History Press
Printed in Great Britain
Manufacturing managed by Jellyfish Print Solutions Ltd

CONTENTS

INTRODUCTION

Deeds of astounding bravery are common in the annals of all three branches of the British armed forces. Unfortunately, most fade into the mists of time, to be recorded in regimental histories or commemorated only by the units involved. However, some military actions have been marked by such courage and devotion to duty that they have found their way into the public's imagination; usually memorialised in books and on film.

On 25 October 1854, following a series of misunderstandings among senior officers, Lord Cardigan led the Light Brigade of British Cavalry along the North Valley at Balaclava in the Crimea, and into the jaws of a 25,000-strong Russian army of cavalry and infantry, supported by batteries of cannon and howitzers. The action was suicidal and ill-fated from the start, and gained no particular tactical advantage. Of the 673 men who are believed to have taken part, about 250 were killed, wounded or taken prisoner. Over 400 horses perished. However, the gallant deeds of the men who responded to orders without question that day are remembered as one of the finest examples of devotion to duty ever performed, and as a result of it the Russians were reluctant to face British cavalry for the remainder of the campaign.

In 1985 I was researching a project about the Battle of Balaclava when I found an article in a Manchester newspaper concerning a benefit concert which had been performed on 21 May 1890, at the Free Trade Hall, to raise funds for the survivors of the Light Brigade who were living in the north of England. Seventeen old campaigners attended the event, which raised nearly £200. I did some follow-up research into the lives of these men, which led me to even more survivors, and the result was the first of a number of articles as biographical tributes that have been forerunners of this work and developed within me a thirst for information on the subject which has never been quenched.

The main aim of this publication is to be factually informative, particularly to the general reader, and unbiased, and while it has been necessary to outline the events leading up to the battle to bring the action into perspective, I have tried to avoid any form of critique concerning the politics of the war, the personalities of the senior officers, and the rights and wrongs of the tactics used on the day. These matters have been covered in most previous books on the subject. The narrative is based on my study of over 100 eyewitness accounts and statements made by the men who actually took part in the action. Some of the accounts differ concerning certain parts of the action of course, some even contradict each other, but I have written the narrative how I see it in my mind's eye, and I have tried to allow readers to form their own opinions.

Over the years I have received the help and valued opinions of prominent historians who spent much of their time studying the subject, including Canon William Lummis (1886–1985), who actually met many of the survivors, Edward James Boys (1916–2002) and David Harvey (1946–2004). I also exchanged information and opinions with the museums of the five regiments involved in the action, descendants of the Light Brigade men, and numerous fellow Light Brigade enthusiasts, including members of The Crimean War Research Society.

I have had many reasons for feeling proud of my British heritage, but never more so than during my time in preparing and writing this book.

Jim Bancroft, Eccles, Salford

1

THE THEATRE OF WAR

'These are deeds which shall not pass
And names that must not wither.'

LORD BYRON

By the middle of the nineteenth century the Turkish Ottoman Empire was falling apart and becoming 'The sick man of Europe'. Britain and France were suspicious of Russia's expansionist intentions in the Balkans, which they considered to be a threat to trade routes. The situation was inflamed when Tsar Nicholas began to interfere in Turkish affairs, prompting the Sultan of Turkey to look towards Britain and France for guidance. Turkey declared war on Russia in October 1853 and Russian forces destroyed a Turkish fleet in the following month. There was a lack of co-operation on both sides, diplomacy broke down and by 27 March 1854 Britain had drifted into war. It was not the first or the last time a British Expeditionary Force was sent across the sea in the defence of a foreign nation's security.

Apart from a number of uprisings within the Empire, the British Army had not been involved in a serious European conflict since the Battle of Waterloo in 1815. The Duke of Wellington had tried to improve the situation for his soldiers by introducing an army pension of a shilling a day for 21 years service, with the option of short service periods up to 12 years. Nevertheless, the military system was precarious and many thought it would eventually break down. There were no reserves and regiments made their own medical arrangements by the use of surgeons who had

'Someone had blundered' – The fact that the Charge of the Light Brigade took place at all was due in no small way to the feuding and petty jealousies of senior officers. Lord Raglan (front left) issued an unclear order that the Russians were to be prevented from capturing a battery of Turkish guns; Captain Nolan (front right) relayed the order with too much haste and without clarifying it; Lord Lucan (rear left) insisted that it was an order from the Commanding Officer and should be carried out without question; and Lord Cardigan (rear right), led his men into the valley of death to attack the enemy positions.

been commissioned into the army. A rudimentary transport and supply system came under the Treasury, restricted by Government economies, and the Commissariat worked on the doctrine that food and transport could be obtained in-theatre. There was no field training and officers recruited through purchased commissions needed only a basic education. Despite all these drawbacks the public considered their army to be invincible – especially the cavalry.

In the 1840s many cavalry regiments were in Ireland policing the terrible effects of the potato famine and maintaining public order during the various insurrections in the strife-torn southern counties. The Duke of Cambridge regularly showcased his cavalry. They were seen on duty throughout the time of the Great Exhibition in Hyde Park in 1851 and most squadrons took part in the funeral of the Duke of Wellington in 1852. Some units served on escort duty when Queen Victoria went on public tours. As war clouds loomed in June 1853, the cavalry took part in a field training exercise on Chobham Common in Surrey; their first for many years. Atrocious weather conditions turned the camp into a muddy quagmire and drenched the miserable troops – a taste of things to come!

Five cavalry regiments formed the Light Brigade, which was sent on active service in the Crimea. For over a century and a half these illustrious units had fought with great distinction on the British Army's many campaigns at home and overseas. The first Dragoon regiment was raised in 1645 for service in Oliver Cromwell's New Model Army to fight in the English Civil War. It is believed that they took their name from the matchlock carbine weapon they used – the dragon – so called because of the dragon's head emblem on the muzzle. Dragoons were originally mounted infantry trained to fight on foot. The horse's only function was to transport the soldier to a place where he could dismount and reinforce the regular infantry. Some Dragoon regiments were adopted for scouting duties, using small men carrying light equipment. These units came to be recognised as elite troops paid at a higher rate than foot soldiers.

The 4th (Queen's Own) Light Dragoons were originally named The Princess Anne of Denmark's Regiment of Dragoons, in honour of King James II's daughter. They were more commonly known as Berkeley's Dragoons, having been raised by Colonel John Berkeley, who had fought with distinction against the Duke of Monmouth's troops at the Battle of Sedgemoor in 1685 and was commissioned to form and

Lord George Paget led the 4th Light Dragoons at Balaclava and was second in command of the Light Cavalry Brigade. A son of the 1st Marquess of Anglesey, he was Member of Parliament for Beaumaris from 1847 to 1857.

command a regiment of independent Dragoons from the Wessex area. The regiment's first campaign was in 1689 when units were sent to Scotland to fight against the Highland clansmen under Bonnie Dundee. They formed part of King William's 'Grand Alliance' in Flanders, 1692–97, confronting the French for the first time at the Battle of Steinkirk in 1692. Battle honours prior to the Crimea were gained at *Dettingen* 1743, during the War of the Austrian Succession; and for their part in the Peninsular War they gained battle honours for *Talavera* 1809, *Albuhera* 1811, *Salamanca* 1812, *Vittoria* 1813, *Toulouse* 1814, and *Peninsula* 1809–14. While serving in India they provided units for the expedition to Afghanistan, gaining battle honours for the storming of *Ghuznee* 1839, and *Afghanistan* 1838–39. The regimental colours are blue with yellow busby bag. Their motto is '*Mente et Manu*' – 'With Heart and Hand', and their nickname is 'Paget's Irregular Horse'. At the Battle of Balaclava they were commanded by Lord George Augustus Frederick Paget, who was second in command of the Brigade. He had recently married, and was the serving Member of Parliament for Beaumaris on the Isle of Anglesey at the time.

The 8th Hussars (King's Royal Irish) were raised after the War of the English Succession, when William of Orange desired to raise a regiment of loyal Irish Protestants who had fought at the Battle of the Boyne in 1690. The unit was raised in Derry, and command was given to Lieutenant-Colonel Henry Cunyngham, who had fought at the Boyne with his father's regiment, the Inniskilling Dragoons, taking the name Cunyngham's Regiment of Irish Dragoons. Battle honours prior to the Crimea were gained while they were serving in India from 1802 to 1822; at *Leswaree* and *Hindustan* 1803. The colours of the regiment are blue with scarlet busby bag, and their motto is *Pristinae Virtutis Memores – The Memory of Former Valour*. At the Battle of Saragossa in 1710, during the War of the Spanish Succession, they captured a regiment of Spanish Horse and appropriated their belts, from which came the inspiration for their nickname 'The Cross Belts'. At the Battle of Balaclava they were commanded by Lieutenant-Colonel Frederick George Shewell.

The 11th Hussars (Prince Albert's Own) were raised by Brigadier-General Philip Honywood as a regiment of Dragoons in the Essex area at the time of the Jacobite Rebellion in 1715. He is believed to have originally mounted them on grey horses. They served during the second Jacobite Rebellion which began in 1745, being present at their only battle on Home soil at Culloden in the following year. They became the 11th Regiment of Dragoons in 1751, converting to Light Dragoons in 1783. Battle honours prior to the Crimea were gained for *Warburg* during the Seven Years War, 1756–63, and *Beaumont* and *Willems* in Flanders 1793–95. The battle honour *Egypt* (with the Sphinx) was gained in 1801, where C Troop particularly distinguished themselves at Alexandria. During the Peninsular War they gained honours at *Salamanca* 1812, and *Peninsula* 1811–13. They served in India from 1819 to 1838, gaining honours during the siege of *Bhurtpore* in 1825. Their colours are blue with crimson busby bag. In recognition that the regiment escorted Prince Albert to the Royal wedding in 1840, Queen Victoria authorised them to become a Hussar regiment, and gave them the unique distinction among cavalry to wear crimson trousers. They adopted the motto in German from the coat of arms of Prince Albert *'Treu Und Fest'* which has variations in English such as Loyal, Faithful or True and Firm, Strong or Steadfast. Lord Cardigan was a former commander of the regiment, and they were commanded at Balaclava by Lieutenant-Colonel John Douglas, who was a close friend of Lord Cardigan. He had even seconded him for in a famous duel in which Cardigan wounded a fellow officer.

The 13th Light Dragoons were raised in the Midlands by Brigadier-General Richard Munden, at the time of the Jacobite Rebellion of 1715, being titled 'Munden's Dragoons'. They also took part in the Jacobite Rebellion in 1745, and in 1751 they adopted the name 13th Regiment of Dragoons, converting to Light Dragoons in 1783. While taking part in the Maroon War in Jamaica, 1796–98, yellow fever almost annihilated the regiment. Battle honours were gained in the Peninsular War at *Albuhera* 1811, *Vittoria* 1813, *Orthes* 1814, *Toulouse* 1814, and *Peninsula* 1811–14. They also gained the honour for the Battle of *Waterloo* 1815. The colours of the regiment are blue with buff collars. Their motto is *Viret in Aeternum*, which in

Officers of the 4th Light Dragoons photographed by Roger Fenton about a year after the Battle of Balaclava. Most of them are wearing blue patrol jackets with black braid and the cavalry forage cap with embroidered peak.

English is *It Flourishes Forever* or *May It Flourish Forever*. Their nickname is 'The Green Dragoons' or 'Evergreens'. At the Battle of Balaclava they were commanded by Captain John Augustus Oldham, who was killed in action.

The 17th Lancers (Duke of Cambridge's Own) were raised in the Home Counties in 1759 by Colonel John Hale of the 47th Regiment, who was a friend of General Wolfe. They were designated the 17th Light Dragoons, and Hale devised the unique 'death's head' badge emblem and the motto *Or Glory*, hence the famous nickname 'The Death or Glory Boys'. When Lancer units came into the British Army after the Battle of Waterloo they replaced the 19th Light Dragoons as the 17th Lancers in 1822. They served in Germany in 1761, and during the American War of Independence they were present at the battles of Bunker's Hill and Brooklyn. They then served in the West Indies for eight years from 1789 to 1797, taking part in the Maroon War in Jamaica. They saw service in South America, 1806-08, and in India from 1808 until 1823. Captain William Morris took command of the regiment on the day of the battle. He was know as 'The Pocket Hercules' because of his short stature and barrel chest, and he had served with distinction in India. He was wounded in action at Balaclava.

At the time of the Crimean War the headdress of Light Dragoons was a black beaver chaco. They wore a dark blue double-breasted tunic which was decorated with gilt and gold chord. The dark blue overalls (trousers) had two gold lace stripes down the outer seam, which indicated that they were light cavalry. However, in the Crimea the 13th were wearing experimental grey trousers. The overalls had no pockets, so the trooper carried a sabretache, which was an elaborately embroidered hanging pouch attached to the sabre belt. These had been discarded for the Crimean campaign. All light cavalry units wore the less bulky ankle boots.

Hussar uniforms generally consisted of a scarlet busby cap, with white plume and red busby bag. Blue-cloth single-breasted jackets were laced and ornamented across the chest with braid. They wore a scarlet waistcoat, and a blue-cloth pelisse (hanging jacket) draped over the left shoulder. When worn, the sabretache was of scarlet embroidered cloth. Hussar units wore blue overalls (except the 11th), and had blue facings.

The 17th Lancers wore a dark blue double breasted jacket and dark blue overalls. However, like the Light Dragoons they were wearing grey trousers in the Crimea. Their headdress was the truncated lancer cap, which was white like their facings. In foul weather they wore a black covering over the helmet.

Light Cavalry carried a steel sword, and 'other ranks' were issued with percussion carbines. Officers carried revolvers, while Troop Sergeant-Majors, trumpeters and Lancers used pistols. Lancers also carried a staff which was nine feet long and made of ash wood. A red and white pennon was attached close to the pointed steel head.

The cavalry commanding officers were all from aristocratic backgrounds aged in their mid-fifties. James Thomas Brudenell, 7th Earl of Cardigan, was given command of the Light Brigade, and his brother-in-law, George Charles Bingham, 3rd Earl of

Lieutenant-Colonel Frederick Shewell led the 8th Hussars during the Light Brigade action at Balaclava. Born in London in 1809, when Lord Cardigan returned to England in January 1855 he took over command of the Light Brigade.

A party of NCOs of the 8th Hussars gather at their cooking house as the cook ladles food into a bowl. Note the woman looking on in the background. The picture was taken by Roger Fenton in 1855.

Lucan, was placed in charge of all the ten regiments which made up the Cavalry Brigade; there being five regiments of heavy cavalry under the command of Sir James Yorke Scarlett – the 1st Dragoons (The Royals), 2nd Dragoons (Scots Greys), 4th Dragoon Guards (Royal Irish), 5th Dragoon Guards (Princess Charlotte of Wales's), and 6th Dragoons (Inniskilling).

During March 1854 cavalry units began to receive orders for active service in the East. TSM George Loy Smith of the 11th Hussars stated: 'An order was issued that all swords were to be collected... to be ground and sharpened... They were not again to be drawn till required, when in presence of the enemy. This little preparation made one think seriously about what was before us, as it looked more like warfare than anything we had before witnessed.' In April the first of over 20 large troop transporters began to leave Plymouth, Portsmouth and Queenstown 'amidst loud acclamations, some of a sorrowful and some of a cheering description', as crowds of people watched their army go off to war in a carnival atmosphere. Thirteen women accompanied their husbands, including Fanny Duberley, the wife of the paymaster of the 8th Hussars, who kept a diary of her experiences: '...as the shores of England faded from our view, we could not help but think of the probabilities of ever returning.'

A group of 17th Lancers pictured in 1856. From left to right: Privates Thomas Smith, William Dimmock, William Pearson and Thomas Foster. They all took part in the Light Brigade action except Smith.

There were a few disasters during the voyages, such as the *Asia* running aground while carrying units of the 11th Hussars. The horses of the 8th Hussars were carried in strong fixed boxes in the hold, with batons to secure them and keep them steady, and there were spare stalls into which the animals could be transferred for cleaning. However, many animals suffered terribly. Horses became frenzied because of the stifling heat in the holds where they were kept close to the ship's engine room. Many stumbled in rough seas and kicked and injured each other as they tried to get back onto their feet. The most serious incident was suffered by the 17th Lancers who lost fifteen mounts when *The Pride of the Ocean* rolled badly in a storm in the Bay of Biscay. The *Simla* was the last transporter to set sail, in mid-July, carrying the 4th Light Dragoons. During the journey the captain of the ship threatened that if a particularly fierce storm they were enduring did not abate very soon they would have to throw all the horses overboard!

As the ships approached Constantinople and the Black Sea the men saw for the first time the hospital building at Scutari, where they would be taken if they were struck down with disease or wounded in battle. Little did they know at that time that it had been built over a cess pool and conditions inside were disgraceful. The floors were rotten and the walls were covered in vermin, with no ventilation. Beds were packed into rooms set out in long lines with little space between them, and there was no clean bedding or clothing. Unbelievably, there were no medical stores, and no cleaning materials or utensils.

The Anglo-French expeditionary force began to disembark at Varna on the east coast of Bulgaria during the last days of May 1854. Most of the cavalry had disembarked by the end of July, and some more horses perished during this difficult procedure, bringing the total of lost mounts to over 50. The 4th Light Dragoons were the last unit to disembark, on 14 August. As the troops began to settle into camp life, the daily routine was to be up at four o'clock in the morning and have everything finished by eight so they could shade from the heat. Much of the time was spent writing letters or anxiously waiting for news from home. Lord Lucan organised field days for his cavalry. However, he used commands that were out-of-date and caused confusion. Lord Paget was obliged to inform Lucan that it was unwise to teach a 'new drill' to men and horses who were due to go into action. To the relief of the cavalry Lucan grudgingly accepted the point.

Sanitary conditions were unhealthy. Rations consisted of rotten biscuits and raw salt pork or beef served on tin plates, with a tot of rum to swill down the odd maggot or two that they had failed to pick out of the food with their grubby fingers. The men were constantly drinking contaminated water. Not surprisingly, dysentery was rife and a cholera epidemic broke out. A man could contract the illness in the morning, spend all day suffering with bad stomach cramps, diarrhoea and vomiting, and be dead and buried by nightfall. The merciless blinding sun beat down on sick and dying men, and two huge hospital marquees were soon filled. By the end of July Surgeon

A contemporary sketch of the exterior buildings at Scutari hospital, which the British Expeditionary Force saw while passing in ships on their way to war. It is the place where the wounded and dying were taken after the Battle of Balaclava. Unfortunately, the hospital was disorganised and filthy, with inadequate supplies and therefore they received only minimal medical attention.

John Crosse of the 11th Hussars was obliged to ask Lord Cardigan to forbid the band from playing the Dead March from *Saul* as it was affecting the morale of the sick and lowering the resistance of men who were capable of possible recovery. Horses were also given bad water and food and as the days went by some began to display the symptoms of glanders, coughing bouts and nasal discharge. Many had to be shot.

The first sounds of hostilities could be heard by the troops at Varna coming from 70 miles to the north-west, as the thud of guns shook the ground when Russian forces attacked the Turkish stronghold at Silistria. On 12 June, Captain Edward Tomkinson took a unit of the 8th Hussars to examine the country up to about 50 miles towards Silistria. He reported a serious scarcity of water and came upon some tracks which he concluded had been left by a body of enemy cavalry about two days previously. The Turks had resisted strongly and rumours of a Russian withdrawal from Silistria reached the British on 22 June. When the report was confirmed three days later Lord Raglan instructed Lord Cardigan to take a cavalry unit consisting of elements of the 8th Hussars and 13th Light Dragoons, totalling just over 200 men, on a scouting mission to the north to see if there were any signs of the Russian army.

Lord Cardigan had taken out a number of previous scouting units, more to demonstrate his desire of an independent command than anything else. The fatigue

force had only three days' rations as it marched through deserted villages all the way
to a place called Trojan's Wall on the banks of the Danube. There they saw and were
seen by the enemy for the first time, when a body of Russian cavalry appeared across
the water. They forced their way back across the wild desert country, where there was
little water and no forage, having to survive on nettles and dock leaves. The patrol
staggered back into Varna seventeen days later, on 9 July. Over 100 horses went
sick for a month due to the deprivations of the journey, and Cardigan was criticised
for taking the patrol on such a long trip when he was ignorant of the terrain. The
mission became notorious as the 'Sore Back' reconnaissance.

Following some confusion and indecisions at headquarters level, it was eventually
decided on 17 August that the expeditionary force was to sail across the Black Sea

Ships in the harbour at Balaclava. On the night of 14–15 November 1854, about 30 of them
floundered in a terrific storm, which caused the loss of most of the stores of warm clothing,
boots and medical supplies.

to invade the Crimean peninsula, the objective being to form a bridgehead and then move south to attack the strategic port of Sebastopol, on the west coast. The exact destination had not been decided upon when the light cavalry began to embark for the trip across the sea in early September. All land transport and ambulances were left at Varna. The final destination of Calamity Bay near Eupatoria having been decided in transit, men of the Royal Navy worked with great zeal as the infantry disembarked without serious incident on 14 September. As Sergeant Smith of the 11th Hussars watched the 'fine fellows' leap onto the beach he thought gravely of how many of them would never leave again, that they were entering the land where their bodies might lie for eternity.

It was strange to see carriages and carts full of Russians, including female civilians, watching the Allied landings from up on the hills above the bay, while no effort was made to resist the invasion. As the British landing crafts approached the shore some officers leading a unit of Cossacks rode down to the beach, dismounted, and began taking notes. They only rode off as the first troops began to disembark.

It took the cavalry nine hours to disembark on 17 September. The horses were lifted out of the hold by harness, placed about sixteen at a time next to their masters on flat-bottomed pontoon boats with ropes to hold them in, and in this way they were towed towards the beach, where the men had to struggle to get their mounts to safety by wading through the last stretch water. Private John Doyle, 8th Hussars, was on one of the first ships to try to land. The vessel carrying him hit a sandbank and the jolt sent him sprawling overboard and he had to swim for his life to the shore. He reached the beach with his headgear and his haversack full of ammunition swamped. The head baker was thrown into the sea too and was lost.

Once they were ashore they set up camp in their drenched clothing as best they could under the circumstances. As darkness fell, units were sent about three miles inland on outpost duty. Not knowing the whereabouts of the enemy, there were many edgy men with nervous trigger fingers, and the very first shots fired at the cavalry in the Crimea were so-called 'friendly fire', when a British scouting party of 11th Hussars came under fire from French soldiers who, in the dark gloom and shadows, mistook them for Russians. The unit quickly dismounted and took shelter behind their saddles and horses, two or three of the chargers being hit, and as there was no retaliatory fire, the French realised it was not the enemy and ceased their firing.

Back at the camp some fires had been lit and the picketed horses were all stood saddled. The men lay within a few paces of their chargers, rolled up in their blankets and cloaks fully dressed with their swords and bridles at hand so they could be mounted and ready for action quickly. Some men had waterproof sheeting to protect them from the elements. At about midnight rifle fire rang out and bullets whizzed through the air above them, and they were soon up and in their saddles on alert. However, it was a false alarm. Apparently a spooked sentry had fired his rifle, which was taken up by the whole picquet line. Lieutenant Alexander Dunn of the 11th

Hussars had a servant who was wearing a long grey coat as he ran to bridle up his master's mount, and in the darkness Lieutenant Robert Annesley, 11th Hussars, mistook him for a Russian and shot him through the thigh.

The Allied army began the march south from the landing site on the morning of 19 September, shadowed by an armada of warships and troop carriers of the British and French Navies sailing parallel to the invasion force. The British took the inland route in two columns, with the Light Brigade providing a screen to the rear with the 4th Light Dragoons, the 8th Hussars and the 17th Lancers protected the left flank, and the 11th Hussars and the 13th Light Dragoons some distance in advance. They had left their valises, palises, spare overalls and boots on board ship, taking with them just a shirt, socks and a towel wrapped in a blanket. They had with them three days provisions of corn and biscuits. The scenery was breathtaking as the army pushed on, but many men were still suffering the ill effects of dysentery and cholera, and as they slogged on under the blistering heat they were visibly weakening. As the humidity sapped their strength they began to discard their equipment and headgear. Many started to fall back, stagger and slump to the ground unable to move or be moved, their canteens empty. It took ten hours to cover the ten miles to the Bulganac River, which, although it was only running about knee deep, provided some relief for their parched throats. Captain William Cresswell, 11th Hussars, died of cholera, having been taken ill whilst on piquet on the night of the 18 September. He was buried in the regiment's bivouac area.

As they approached the river, men of the Light Brigade eyed the high ground across the water and saw Cossack scouts, who fell back each time the Allied advance got too near to them. Lord Raglan ordered Lord Cardigan to reconnoitre across the river to find out the strength of the enemy in that direction. As he reached the crest of some high ground on the other side of the water and looked across a long valley, he saw the main body of the Cossack unit spread out in skirmishing order about a mile away. It was here that the Russians witnessed the fearless attitude of the British cavalry for the first of many times. They descended the hill, with 13th Light Dragoons skirmishers ahead of them, and moved across the valley through a melon field towards the enemy, which was at least twice their number in strength. They halted about 200 paces from the Cossack line.

The first shot of the campaign was fired when a Cossack in front of the 11th Hussars raised his carbine and pulled the trigger, and the whole line then opened fire. The British were ordered to exchange fire and draw swords, and, even though the crest of the hill behind the Cossack line became alive with enemy troops which 'lit up with the glitter of swords and lances', they were boldly moving towards the Russians up an incline at the trot and ready to charge. However, an ADC brought a message from Lord Raglan ordering the cavalry to retire. The commander had advanced to the hill behind them and through field glasses he could see a force of 6000 enemy waiting behind the hill to the front, which had been sent forward from their main positions on the Alma ridge and was hidden from Lord Lucan's view. A Russian battery began to send round shot 'bounding like cricket balls' at them, and a unit of infantry had formed square in readiness to receive the charge. Private William Pennington, 11th Hussars, recalled: 'Some of us more nervous fellows were bowing our heads over our horse's manes.' Which caused Major Edmund Peel of his regiment to remonstrate in an angry tone: 'What the hell are you bobbing your heads at?' However, British artillery and the 8th Hussars and 17th Lancers came up in support and Cardigan was able to retire his men in alternate troops as if on a field day exercise back in Britain.

The first British casualties of the war through enemy action, human and equine, were suffered by the Light Brigade. Among the 13th Light Dragoons, Private George Badger was wounded in the foot, and a grey horse was killed when it was hit by an exploding shell, but its rider, Private James Shaw, was spared. However, the blast took away Sergeant Joseph Priestley's foot and he became the first man to suffer 'the smart

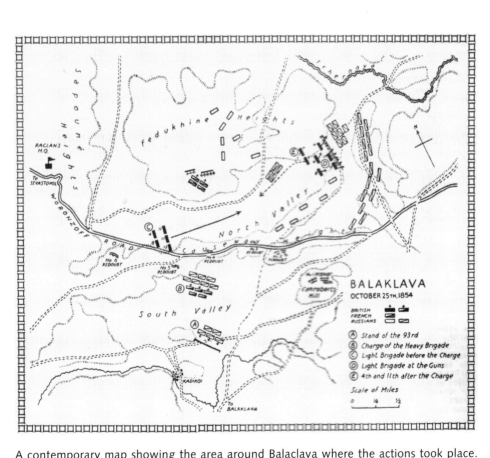

A contemporary map showing the area around Balaclava where the actions took place. The Light Brigade was drawn up to the west end of the North Valley before they advanced eastward into a mass of Russian firepower to their front, and on the flanking hills.

of the knife' when he had to have his leg amputated in the field. Private William Nicholson's charger was hit by a shell and blown out of the ranks, causing the saddle to slip round its body and tip the trooper onto the floor, before the horse ran away with his saddle and cloak. He never saw either item again. The 11th Hussars also received casualties. Private James Williamson rode up to his troop leader, Lieutenant Roger Palmer, with his foot dangling loosely from a serious wound which was gushing blood, and announced in a matter-of-fact way: 'Sir, I am hit. May I fall out?' Private John Henry had his foot shot off and the wound mortified during the next few weeks causing his death.

Queen Victoria had recently permitted the use of chloroform for the birth of her seventh child, thereby endorsing the use of anaesthetics, but its use on the battlefield was determined by the opinions and experience of the medical staff present and its availability.

On returning to the hill from where they had started, the Light Brigade dismounted near the crest, where a sack of biscuits and a stone bottle of rum were distributed among them. The enemy Cossacks jeered at them as they were forced to retire and they were disgruntled at having been held back. It was from this time that Lord Lucan unfairly began to suffer the nickname 'Lord Look-on!' Lord Cardigan fared better as Lord Raglan's dispatch stated: 'Major-General the Earl of Cardigan exhibited the utmost spirit and coolness, and kept his brigade under perfect command.'

The whole army bivouacked in order of battle, and next day, 20 September 1854, they moved the seven miles south along the coast road and across open rolling grassland towards the River Alma, where Prince Alexander Menshikov had been sent out from Sebastopol with over 40,000 infantry and cavalry and 122 guns, to hold back the invasion force and make a stand from a commanding and intimidating position on some high cliffs overlooking the river. The position was considered impregnable and the Russians were so confident they could hold back the Allies that they constructed observation towers from where they intended to watch Allied movements for several weeks. Several ladies of the town had also come out to watch the events, wrapped in their shawls and holding parasols.

The main body of the enemy force was situated directly in front of the British Army's centre, covered by a battery of eight heavy siege guns at the front of its position, known as the Great Redoubt. That afternoon young men and youths fresh from Britain marched towards the elevated enemy positions and the Light Brigade guarded the inland flanks and rear. After the Russians had set fire to the contents of the huts in a village on the banks of the river to try to mask where the Russian guns were situated and cause some confusion to the advancing British ranks, the battery of heavy guns opened fire with considerable effect as the infantry began to cross the river and worked their way over and through numerous obstacles, which caused them to become disorganised. Unable to regroup their troops under fire and the blankets of smoke, British officers urged their men to attack. They surged forward and opened fire on the Russians, driving them back, but they were forced to withdraw down the hill as casualties mounted and a large body of Russian infantry approached for a counter-attack. 'Still, nothing could stop that renowned infantry.' Two nine-pounder guns were brought up to support a renewed attack. Moving up the hill, firing as they advanced, the British were able to retake the Great Redoubt after heavy fighting. British infantry on the summit of the hills were quickly joined by artillery, which began firing into the retreating Russian troops. By late afternoon the Allied victory was complete.

The Light Brigade played mainly a protective role on the left flank of the army during the battle. At one point a large unit of Russian cavalry manoeuvred into position as if they were preparing to charge the British infantry on the left flank. Officers bellowed out orders and the Light Brigade then wheeled about to face it, and extended into single line to create the image that there were more of them, with the intention of attacking the Russian horsemen in their flank if they attempted to charge. When the battle was won and the Russians were retreating in disorder the 11th Hussars and 17th Lancers were ordered to pursue them and make prisoners of any stragglers. They crossed the river, their thirsty horses not being allowed to stop and drink, and beyond the river some mounts became entangled in the foliage of trees in vineyards and gardens, and they were badly impeded by the bodies of dead and wounded men. They ascended the Heights with the Highlanders, and as the 17th Lancers galloped across the front of the lines of Highlanders, Colin Campbell's gruff voice boomed out and they were soundly told off for disrupting the momentum as his men surged forward. The Light Brigade was eventually ordered to check their advance and hold back by Lord Raglan.

Several acts of treachery were performed by the enemy during the pursuit. TSM George Loy Smith, 11th Hussars, noticed a Russian lying on the ground apparently dead. However, as the artillery clattered forward ahead of the cavalry he rolled onto his side, produced a rifle he had been hiding under his body, and shot one of the men riding at the back of a gun-carriage. He was despatched by a cavalry trooper as he rode by, but the Artilleryman was badly wounded. Sergeant Seth Bond, 11th Hussars, came face-to-face with a Russian who pretended to surrender. However, as the prisoner was supposedly giving up his weapon he made a bayonet thrust into Bond's face. The sergeant was about to retaliate and cut the Russian down when an officer rode up and told him to spare the 'scoundrel'. Private James Wightman, 17th Lancers, confronted a Russian officer, who fired his hand gun at him from close range and took away one of the rings of his horse's bit. Wightman reined in on him, smashed him to the ground with the butt of his lance, and marched him back as a prisoner of war, where Colonel Lawrenson called him a coward for his defensive action! Although the Light Brigade had been under cannon and rifle fire on several occasions, Sergeant Bond and Private George Dunn of the 17th Lancers were the only cavalrymen to receive a wound during the battle.

As the exhausted soldiers tried to sleep out in the open that night with grass for bedding and stones as pillows, the air was soured by a sickening stench of blood and rotting flesh. All around them the spine-chilling cries of injured and dying men echoed in their ears. Some asked for a drink of water to quench their unbearable thirst, while many souls prayed to their God for the last time and begged for someone to come and put them out of their misery. Some could see their own limbs lying close by, in ground soaked by their own blood. These disturbing sights and sounds had a bad effect on even the most hardened men as they came to realise that if they found themselves in the same situation they could expect little help at a time when they needed it most.

British casualties were over 2000, and for three days the Allies buried their dead and tended to their wounded; most of whom were sent on board ships bound for Scutari without first having their injuries tended to by a medic. Burial detachments picked a square plot in which to dig a pit, and unceremoniously dragged in as many bodies at it would hold. It was rich pickings for the scavenger birds that hovered overhead or swooped down to make snatches at the corpses before they had been covered with soil. In some cases they had already pecked a man's body to the bone as it lay in the open.

The march south towards Sebastopol resumed on 23 September.

The Lancers considered Colonel Lawrenson to be: '…a little too extra-dainty for the rough-and-ready business of warfare.' He had been doubled up with pain during the Battle of the Alma and the next day he went home sick. Major Augustus Willett: 'a good soldier, but a tyrant', took over command of the regiment. Lord Raglan asked for an escort of 8th Hussars, so Captain George Chetwode and 40 men were assigned to this duty. Following a report that Russian troops escorting baggage wagons had been seen at McKenzie's Farm on the supply road from Sebastopol to Symferopol, and the unit of 8th Hussars were among the cavalry thrown out in skirmishing order towards them. Horse Artillery opened fire, causing the Russians to abandon all their wagons and flee from the scene. The cavalry chased after the Russian baggage guard, who sent a volley over their heads and rode off. Seventy wagons and a large quantity of baggage fell into British hands, including some of Prince Menshikov's personal belongings. The troops were allowed to pillage the wagons that did not contain anything of value to the Commissariat, and Trumpeter William Smith, 11th Hussars, acquired an engraved silver punch ladle, which Lord Lucan requested to see, but did not return!

On 25 September the cavalry made camp in the Tchernaya Valley, about four miles north-east of Balaclava, where TSM Loy Smith saw two Cossack scouts on the hills watching their movements. On the following day they continued their trek south, marching over the Traktir Bridge and onto the Balaclava plain, divided into a north and south valley by the Causeway Heights, which carried the main track up to a plateau to the west, beyond which was the town of Sebastopol. As they moved across the eastern end of the north valley many a man was unknowingly riding over his own grave. They marched over the Causeway and across the south valley, and as they moved through the village of Kadikoi they came under fire, a few shells from a small fort near the mouth of Balaclava harbour. A quick response from the Royal Navy prompted a white flag to be raised and the harbour was soon in the hands of the invasion force.

The cavalry bivouacked just outside Kadikoi, close to some beautiful gardens and vineyards full of luscious grapes, on which all ranks made a raid. There was plenty of water, hay, corn and wood for fuel. After three nights exposed to the elements on the Balaclava plain the Heavies lent the Lights some tents. The united cavalry brigades formed various patrols by day and picquets and outposts at night, while the Turks erected six earthworks on the Causeway Heights, under the guidance of the British cavalry. The Naval Brigade then installed some naval guns.

Supplies began to get scarce as they entered October, and as the nights turned cold wooden buildings were pulled down so the materials could be used as fuel for warmth and to cook food and boil water. A trooper of the 8th Hussars remembered that his unit had nothing but salt meat to eat for seven consecutive days, and every man was thankful for the tot of rum ration to mask the awful taste. The Cavalry and Artillery were almost always mounted and formed up in front of the lines an hour before daybreak until reports from outposts came in. The Cavalry scouted east and around the area of the Tchernaya, and soon began to encounter Russian patrols; but there were no confrontations. In mid-October, Captain Robert White, 17th Lancers, was on outlying picquet on the Kamara Hills when he reported that he had observed a large force of Russian cavalry. In fact, up to 23 October, all the Russian cavalry was in bivouac on the Kacha River, some three miles from the town of Bakhchisarai, and each day it sent squadrons out on various scouting expeditions.

On 13 October, Captain Oldham and a unit of 16 men of his regiment were ordered to proceed to the River Tchernaya, to gain intelligence about the Russians on the opposite bank. Sergeant Henry Alderson and four men were told to ride ahead and advance to the river. They crossed the bridge and as they moved up a hill on the opposite side, four Russian hussars rode out from the trees and three more came over the top of the hill and gave chase. The sergeant turned to his left and rode alongside the hill. However, this was towards the Russian camp and his pursuers closed in on him and he was taken prisoner.

By 21 October the Allies had advanced so close to the walls of Sebastopol that they could hear their bands playing polkas and marches. That evening was bitter cold and there was an icy wind, and intelligence was received that a large Russian force was marching on Balaclava from the east. The cavalry was ordered to stand to horses, where they remained on alert for fourteen hours. For reasons known only to him, Major Willett would not wear an overcoat, and he would not allow any of his officers or men to wear a cloak. Apparently, some officers denounced the practice as 'effeminate'. However, he became a victim of his own stubborn rule when he died of exposure. Captain William Morris – 'The Pocket Hercules' – took command of the 17th Lancers.

Old campaigners such as Corporal John Penn of the 17th Lancers, who was out on picket duty, used an old trick he had learned while serving in Afghanistan and India by putting his ears to the ground and detecting the tramp of horses hoofs and the rumble of gun wheels, which suggested there was an army on the move somewhere in the distance. As the fateful day approached Lord Paget had written in his diary: 'Very quiet here today and no alarms.' The lull before one of the most famous storms in the history of British arms.

2

ENEMY ONSLAUGHT

'Oh, war, war! The details of it are horrid.'

LORD GEORGE PAGET

Wednesday, 25 October 1854 (13 October to the Russians), was St Crispin's Day, and the anniversary of the Battle of Agincourt, when the English army won a great victory over the French for Henry V. The Cavalry Division was standing to horses at 5.30am, on alert in front of their camp at Kadikoi, with their front facing Canrobert's Hill, a mile-and-a-half to the east. There were groans from the ranks because they had got wet from a rainstorm during the night; they were waiting for the order to return to their lines to have breakfast and get properly dried. Unknown to them, at about the same time the Russian army was moving south to attack Balaclava, in an attempt to cut off the British army's line of supply and break the siege of Sebastopol by attacking the Allies from their rear.

Some time later Lord Lucan rode by with a small party of staff officers on his regular inspection of the outposts, so Lord Paget mounted and joined the entourage. There was a mist in the air, but the dim light of dawn was beginning to appear on the crest of the hills beyond the Causeway, illuminating the skyline. As they cantered across the plain towards Canrobert's Hill, the redoubt positions along the Causeway were becoming vaguely visible, and a confused look crossed the face of Lord William Paulett as he looked towards a warning flagstaff which had been raised on the previous day. He had noticed that two flags were flying. On pointing this out to the other officers, Major Thomas McMahon replied: 'Why surely, that is the signal that the enemy are approaching.' Their perplexity was dispelled almost at once when the guns from one of the redoubts thundered and there was intense activity as the videttes circled backwards and forwards all along the Causeway. The ground began to shake as the cannonades increased, and it was reported that Russian cavalry was advancing towards them from the north-east, supported by a large force of infantry. A sense of urgency prevailed and Lord Paget galloped back to his Brigade.

Lord Raglan received intelligence from Lord Lucan and French HQ that a patrol had sighted 'a large Russian force threatening Balaclava'. French artillery on the plateau opened fire over the heads of the cavalry division towards the north valley where a strong body of Russian cavalry was advancing. At 8 o'clock, Fanny Duberly was on board a ship in the harbour when she received a scribbled note from her husband, Henry, stating: 'The battle of Balaclava has begun and promises to be a hot one. I send you the horse. Lose no time but come up as quickly as you can; do not wait for breakfast.' Frances rushed ashore and quickly mounted the horse on which she galloped up towards the south valley. There she met a Commissariat officer who told her that the Russians were attacking in force and their cavalry had even advanced into the south valley chasing down the Turks who had abandoned their positions. He yelled a warning as she cantered off westward: 'For God's sake ride fast, or you may not reach the camp alive!'

The men in the cavalry lines had also heard the thud of cannon fire and there was much speculation of action at last from the troopers. Lord Paget came spurring out of the shadows, and almost at once the order rang out to mount. Soon afterwards an ADC from Lord Lucan arrived and delivered the order that the Cavalry Division was to advance to support the Turkish troops preparing to defend the gun positions on the Causeway Heights. Colonel Douglas summed up the mood when he addressed his men as they prepared for battle: 'In all probability we shall meet the enemy today. When you do, don't cut but give them the point, and they will never face you again.' This was sound advice from him. Captain John Platt Winter had his arm in a sling from a badly injured finger and he was asked by his men not to get involved in the battle. His loyal and encouraging reply was a defiant: 'Where my men go, I go.'

The Cavalry Brigade, and I Troop, Royal Artillery, moved out and off onto the plain. The vineyard impeded the progress of the Artillery guns, but they pressed forward towards a point a little way to the right of number 3 redoubt. The Artillery moved up the slope and was brought into action as they reached the top. The Light Brigade were halted to the left of number 2 redoubt, and the Heavy Brigade placed themselves across a pass between number 2 redoubt and Canrobert's Hill. Both Brigades were below the ridge of the Causeway. To their rear, Major-General Sir Colin Campbell's 93rd Highlanders had marched up from Kadikoi and took up a position close to the track from Balaclava, as a last line of defence to protect the route down to the harbour.

By this time Russian forces were massing in the north valley and infantry were assaulting Canrobert's Hill. They were also moving into positions to try to take the rest of the redoubts along the defensive line. The sun was now well above the horizon and its bright rays were dazzling the Artillery gunners, making it difficult to see the enemy. The Russian cannonades seemed to be directed at the number 3 redoubt, and I Troop could only reply by aiming at the line of flashes along the Fedioukine Heights, the enemy guns being masked behind the sun's glare. The Russian assault was ferocious and their fierce shouts could be heard from the British cavalry lines. General Scarlett detached the Scots Greys to support Turkish resistance. By this time the Russian artillery had found the range of the British front lines and their ordnance rained down on what was an easy target. The round shot and shell came whizzing over the hill, some bouncing with speed toward the British. Terrible casualties were being sustained, especially among the Artillery and their horses. The men started to move their heads from side-to-side trying to dodge the shells, but the officers assured them that such a reaction would not help them to avoid a 32-pound shell and they were just as likely to be moving their heads into its path as out of it. Some of them did – a dreadful sight to see.

Lord Paget had a couple of narrow escapes. He was out in front of the Brigade watching the movement of the enemy when a shell burst close in front of him and

Sir James Yorke Scarlett led from the front swirling his sabre in the air during the charge of the Heavy Brigade at Balaclava. He died in 1871, aged 72, and he is buried in Holme Chapel, Cliviger near Burnley.

a splinter from it hit his stirrup. On asking his orderly, Private Samuel Parkes, what it was, Parkes replied, 'It was a piece of shell, my Lord. It nearly took your foot off!' Wanting it as a souvenir of war, his Lordship shouted to Parkes: 'Well pick it up and take care of it. I shall send it Home to England!' Soon afterwards a spent cannon ball came bouncing at him and passed right under his horse. Private Parkes was amused by this and laughed: 'Ha-ha! It went right between your horse's legs.' Paget was annoyed at his audacity, and replied: 'Well you seem to think it a good joke, but I don't see anything to laugh at.'

Soon after this, Parkes also had a lucky escape when he returned to the ranks to light his pipe. He was holding the light inside his shako and standing to the side of a horse's head to shield the flame. A round shot zoomed over the hill, bounced on the ground about 20 paces in front of the regiment, bounded into the ranks, and thumped into the neck of the horse next to which Parkes was sheltering, taking away its head. The carcass of the animal was left upright for a short while, then its legs folded and the body smashed to the ground, leaving Sam standing dazed but unharmed.

A cannon ball exploded and sprayed the 13th Light Dragoons with fragments of jagged metal debris. Captain Thomas Goad saw his brother, Cornet George, hit. His horse swirled around and as it crashed to the ground it rolled on him, injuring him severely. A rough-haired terrier puppy named Jemmy, which had been brought on active service by Private Martin Lennon of the 8th Hussars, was scampering about following the spent shot and shell and snapping at fuses. A shell landed under the horse of Captain Charles Longmore of the 8th Hussars but before it exploded the little dog pounced on it and pulled out the fuse with its teeth, thus saving the lives of both man and horse.

Canrobert's Hill was overrun by the Russians in a short time; as enemy infantry began to assault the other redoubts, the sight of their comrades fleeing from their positions had a devastating effect on the Turks all along the Causeway and resistance began to break down. Seeing that the Artillery was being outgunned by superior numbers and their ammunition was almost expended, Lord Lucan gave the order for them to retire, which they did, leaving about a third of their horses behind as casualties. Very soon the slopes of the Causeway came alive with fleeing Turkish troops, and their banners were soon replaced by Tsarist flags. As they streamed down the slopes laden with kit and blankets and reached the plain below, a unit of Cossack horsemen swept around the hill and attacked them with lances and slashing sabres. Some raised their arms and pleaded to be spared, only to have them sliced off. However some: 'Johnny Turks' fought back, and one was seen to turn and face two mounted Cossack adversaries with his weapon loaded and his bayonet fixed. He shot one off his horse and thrust his bayonet into the other, before moving off across the plain at a leisurely walking pace.

As Turkish troops were running towards the British lines, shouting 'Ship, Johnny! Ship, Johnny!' the cavalry fell back in alternate squadrons to cover their retreat;

The Scots Greys rode their chargers headlong against the Russian horsemen and cut their way through the first ranks, and against all odds they got the better of the struggle through sheer guts and determination. Sir Colin Campbell, who himself had just led his 'Thin Red Line' in a successful action against enemy cavalry, congratulated his fellow Scots: 'Greys, gallant Greys! I am sixty-one years old, and if I were young again I should be proud to be in your ranks!'

several horses of the Scots Greys were killed as they did so. The Heavies were forced to gallop over their struck tents and belongings, which had not been packed away. The Turks also passed through the British cavalry camp, rifling their possessions and stealing anything they could find that was edible. The Turks came rushing along the path down to Balaclava just as Fanny Duberly was riding out of the gorge. She became furious on witnessing their retreat and gave them mouthfuls of abuse and hit some of them with her clenched fist to try to get them to stand their ground. She managed to reach the Sapouné Heights without any further incident.

The Russians turned the captured naval guns around and sent barrages down across the south valley, as more Russian batteries were being hastily brought up and placed along the captured positions. The French batteries on the plateau to the west were still firing over the heads of the men in the Cavalry Division, and as this was happening a voice rang out: 'Scarlett, look to your left.' On doing so, the commander saw that there was a large force of enemy Hussars and Cossacks, over 4000 strong, and formed up in close columns of squadrons, riding over the Causeway. They came on down the slope of the hill in good order, moving slowly at first before breaking into a canter and proceeding to advance across the south valley towards the British cavalry lines. I Troop fired a few salvos at the advancing enemy then retired on the cavalry.

Sir Colin had positioned his six companies of Highlanders numbering about 500 men in two ranks on the crest of some slightly rising ground which ran across the entrance to a gorge beyond which was the harbour at Balaclava. They had been joined by 30 or 40 men, including some men of the Guards Brigade, who had volunteered to come up from Balaclava to reinforce the Highlanders. Some of the retreating Turks regained their nerve when they saw the line of Scots with fixed bayonets, and they formed up on each flank. Wearing red tunics, green and black tartan kilts, and black bonnets with a white plume, some men in the line began to fall, one man having his leg blasted away by a round shot, so Campbell ordered them to fall back a few paces and lie on their stomachs on the far slope, in the hope that the hill would give them some protection.

As the mass of Russian cavalry moved across the plain, a section of about 400 Hussars in light-blue uniforms veered to their left away from the main body and began to advance directly at the Highlanders. It was a critical moment, as Balaclava was now under serious threat from the enemy. If the Highlanders faltered the supply harbour would certainly fall into enemy hands. As this body of horsemen broke into a charge, Sir Colin rode along the 'thin red streak tipped with steel' and yelled at them in earnest: 'Men, remember there is no retreat from here. You must die where you stand!' Realising this was indeed the situation, many of his men shouted back: 'Aye, Sir Colin, we'll do that!' However, on these words the Turks lost their nerve and began to move off from the line and make their way down to the harbour. The commander then ordered his men to step up to the crest of the hill, where the front rank dropped down onto one knee. They presented their rifles and steadied themselves.

When the enemy Hussars were only about 50 paces away they fired a volley. As the bullets hit them and men fell from their horses, the Russian cavalrymen faltered at first, and then they moved even more to their left. They veered and wheeled about in an attempt to outflank the Scots on the left of the line. Captain Ross of the Grenadier Company saw the danger and on hastily manoeuvring his men further to the right, he ordered them to fire a second volley. As the line of muskets fired the slugs stopped the enemy horses in their tracks and they began to fall back. Some of the Highlanders started to edge forward, wanting to dash out of the ranks and engage the cavalry on foot with cold steel, but Sir Colin needed them to stand fast and he was heard shouting sternly: 'Ninety-third! Ninety-third! Damn all that eagerness.' One more volley was enough to stop the Russian Hussars in their tracks and they began retreating to their cavalry lines. The Highlanders burst into cheers as Balaclava was safe for the time being. However, they could not stand down because units of Cossack riders were marauding across the plain. Some even came into the camp of the Light Cavalry ransacking any belongings they could find and slashing at the spare horses, causing terrible wounds.

The Heavy Brigade had been ordered to form column of troops in support of the Highlanders but they had not had chance to complete the movement before the Russian cavalry had appeared. The enemy's leading line was about three times the extent of the Heavy Brigade, and three times as deep; behind that was another line equally formidable in numbers. As they came to within a few hundred yards they suddenly halted. Taking advantage of this tactical error, General Scarlett ordered his Brigade to 'wheel into line', and ordered his trumpeter to sound the charge.

As the waves of British horses thundered into action, Scarlett was way ahead of his Brigade, waving his sword above his head, with his ADC, Alexander Elliott, his orderly and a trumpeter not far behind. Behind them was the Adjutant, Alexander Miller, famous for his howling voice, who was leading the two squadrons of Scots Greys and a squadron of the Inniskillings. They extended to one line as they advanced, and the Greys gave out a fierce moan which echoed across the valley. Their large, cumbersome chargers barged the enemy horses out of the way as they slammed into them, the riders slashing left and right and thrusting with their sabres, and the Inniskillings cheered as they met the centre of the Russian line. There was the clash of steel on steel as the frenzied British with glaring, determined eyes and faces paled with rage smashed their way through the wall of stunned Russians, who brought forward their flanks on each side in an effort to encircle the Heavies. The 2nd Squadron of the Inniskillings, followed by the 4th and 5th Dragoon Guards and the Royals, brushed their way through the vineyard, scaled two fences, then rode up a bank and leaped over a ditch, leaving them little space in which to gather the momentum for an all-out charge. They had not formed up in good order for the attack. That great horse 'Peter

Sergeant-Major John Grieve and Sergeant Henry Ramage of the Scots Greys were awarded the Victoria Cross for their gallantry during the Charge of the Heavy Brigade at Balaclava. Sergeant-Major Grieve saw that one of his officers had been surrounded and rode up to assist him. He dispatched the first Russian he encountered and the rest of the assailants dispersed. Sergeant Ramage saw Private McPherson in great peril from an attack by as many as seven Russians and galloped into action to disperse them and save his life.

Simple' had won its second Grand National the previous year over a less hazardous course. As they crashed into the enemy ranks they slashed with their swords, which in many cases just bounced off the thick Russian greatcoats, so with their bridle hands they grabbed at loose reins to try to unbalance the enemy troops and pull them out of their saddles, while some resorted to fisticuffs and several Russian horsemen were on the receiving end of thumps the like of which the national pugilist hero, Tom Sayers, would have been proud.

Meanwhile the Greys and Inniskillings had cut their way through the first line of enemy ranks and although their numbers were depleted and they were in disorder, against all odds they were getting the better of the struggle through sheer determination. As they found themselves in the open space between the lines of enemy cavalry, some Russians fell out of rank among the jostling horsemen and tried to overwhelm them. Sergeant-Major John Grieve of the Scots Greys saw that one of his officers had been surrounded in this way and rode up to assist him. He slashed at the first Russian he encountered and cut off his head, and at the sight of this gruesome spectacle the rest of the assailants dispersed. Sergeant Henry Ramage saw that Private McPherson had been severely wounded and was in great peril from an attack by as many as seven Russians and galloped into action. He hit out at every man who was wearing a Russian greatcoat until they too dispersed.

Lieutenant Miller then roared out of the confused mass and shouted: 'Rally – The Greys face me!' It was a nervous time for the onlookers as the Greys and Inniskillings formed up again as best they could and raced into the second line. Many thought that the Brigade was lost until grey horses and red coats began to emerge from the rear of the second line and immediately fought their way back into the entangled mass. By this time the Russian nerve had been broken and they began to turn and retire in disorder. While this was happening, Sergeant Ramage tried to spur his horse after a Russian but it refused to move. Cursing his horse as he dismounted, Ramage chased down and confronted the Russian on foot, bringing him in as a prisoner. The Russians eventually retreated back around the number 1 redoubt to rejoin their main army.

Eight men of the Heavy Brigade had been killed and 70 were wounded. General Scarlett had received five slight sword cut wounds and had his helmet cloven through. ADC Elliott had received 14 cuts to his body. Among the wounded was Cornet Grey Neville, the 24-year-old son of Lord Braybrook. He died of his wounds at Scutari, and his brother, Henry, was killed while fighting with the Grenadier Guards at Inkerman. As the victorious men in the Brigade sat exchanging stories and congratulating each other on a job well done, a Staff Officer rode up and announced: 'I am ordered by Lord Raglan to say well done, Scarlett!' and Sir Colin Campbell rode up in triumph and congratulated his fellow Scots: 'Greys, gallant Greys! I am 61 years old, and if I were young again I should be proud to be in your ranks!' Scotland had indeed been brave that morning.

There followed a lull in the action. Lord Raglan looked eastwards from his elevated vantage point on the Sapouné Heights just above the rear of the line of the Cavalry Brigade, the noises of their restless horses snorting and stamping their hoofs audible from below the ridge. The Heavy Brigade was drawn up to the right rear of the Light Brigade, and a unit from the French army of Africa known as the Chasseurs de Afrique, 'Huntsmen of Africa', was situated to their left rear, at quite some distance away. They wore light blue tunics tucked into a red sash, and baggy red overalls. Known as 'The Travellers', they had vast experience of hunting and fighting in the hot climate in Algeria and in the hills of Morocco.

Lord Raglan had a panoramic view across the valley, where Russian forces had re-grouped. General Ryzhov concentrated his units on the Fedioukine Hills to the north of the valley, which included horse artillery and four battalions of rifle sharpshooters, some of whom had placed themselves in rifle pits, and Russian forces were positioning themselves on the Causeway to the right. Colonel, Prince Obolensky had placed a field battery of eight six-pounder cannon in a commanding defensive position across the far end of the valley, and manned them with Don Cossacks. These were supported by several units of Lancers, and the 14 squadrons of Hussars that had been repulsed by the Heavy Brigade. The total force was 20,000 infantry and 5,000 cavalry. The Odessky Regiment, with supporting ancillaries, was ordered to move forward along the Causeway to the most western of the captured redoubts to begin removing the British naval guns. Lord Raglan had already sent an order to Lucan stating: 'Cavalry to advance and take advantage of any opportunity to recover the Heights. They will be supported by infantry which have been ordered to advance on two fronts.'

However, as they scanned the valley, this became a matter of urgency when the Staff looked through field glasses and saw great activity on the Turkish redoubts. Limbers were being brought up and it was suggested: 'They are going to take away the guns.' The Commander-in-Chief was alarmed, as this was the equivalent of an infantry battalion having its colours captured by the enemy. The British infantry was not yet in position to prevent this from happening and the only troops on hand were the cavalry, 600 feet below the ridge; who were also waiting for the infantry to arrive. Lord Raglan turned to Quartermaster-General, Sir Richard Airey, and gave instructions, which the QMG quickly scribbled down: 'Lord Raglan wishes the cavalry to advance rapidly to the front – follow the enemy and try to prevent the enemy carrying away the guns – Troop Horse Artillery may accompany – French cavalry is on your left – immediate.'

Lord Raglan intended the order to be read as following up his previous written order and he needed the note to be conveyed safely and with speed. He therefore instructed his Aide: 'Send Nolan.' The 'bit of paper' was entrusted to one of the finest horsemen in the cavalry, Captain Lewis Edward Nolan of the 15th Hussars, to take to Lord Lucan. Nolan was a cavalry fanatic who was agitated because the Light Brigade had not been used and the battle seemed to be over. As he set off Raglan added words that were music to his ears: 'Tell Lord Lucan the Cavalry is to attack immediately.' Captain Nolan had no intention of allowing the two 'dithering' cavalry commanders to delay matters any longer and he responded: 'I'll lead them myself! I'll lead them on!' He eased his grey Arab charger over the edge of the ridge and began to guide it down the precipitous slope, slithering and recovering as he descended. He arrived safely at the bottom, where he and a French officer proceeded to reconnoitre the area to make sure the cavalry would not run into a trap when he delivered the order and they began to carry it out.

All this time, Lord Cardigan had been seated on his chestnut horse, Ronald, which he had personally selected to be his charger. He had kept his men standing to horses in ranks across the end of the north valley on rising ground below the Sapouné Heights, facing directly down the valley, where the terrain immediately in front of them was rocky and broken up. The 11th Hussars, 13th Light Dragoons and 17th Lancers formed the front line of the Brigade, while the second line consisted of the

4th Light Dragoons and the 8th Hussars. The men were becoming frustrated at being deliberately held back and although several officers had urged him to allow them to attack the flank of the retreating Russians, Cardigan would accept no counsel from his subordinates.

Captain Morris was convinced that they would take the opportunity to charge the flank of the retreating Russian cavalry and he started to prepare his men for the attack by breaking away from the main body of the Brigade. The Lancers began to wheel about to face the enemy. Lord Cardigan saw this happening and with a disgruntled tone of voice he asked Captain Morris what he was doing. Captain Morris was equally indignant, and questioned his commander: 'My Lord, are you not going to charge the fleeing enemy?'

'No. We have orders to remain here.' Cardigan replied.

'But, my Lord, It is our positive duty to follow up this advantage.' Captain Morris protested.

'No, we must remain here!' Cardigan insisted.

Captain Morris shook his head in disbelief: 'Do, my Lord, allow me to charge them with the seventeenth. See, my Lord, they are in disorder.'

Lord Cardigan was adamant, and retorted: 'No, no, sir, we must not stir from here.' He ordered Morris to get his men to fall back into column.

Captain Morris turned to Captain Godfrey Morgan and the other officers who were in earshot and fumed: 'Gentlemen, you are witnesses to my request.' Slapping the flat

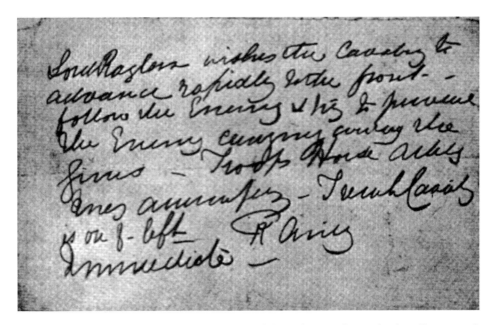

The hastily written, contentious note that doomed the Light Brigade to take the offensive and charge down the north valley.

of his sabre blade against the side of his leg he growled: 'My God, my God, what a chance we are losing!'

Eyes looked down from the hills all around on the 670 cavalrymen who had turned up for duty that day. They had taken little part in the battle so far and they were furious that their section of 'the finest cavalry brigade that ever left the shores of England' had not been used in an independent action. The men who had managed to save some rations were enjoying biscuits, meat and hard boiled eggs, none of which was palatable. Some had a tot of rum to disguise the horrible taste. Private Thomas Hefferon had been badly affected during the 'Soreback' ride and had only recently returned to duty, having expressed his surprise at the severity of the enemy fire. He, Private Lennon and Private John Doyle were enjoying some rations of biscuit and pieces of pork which Doyle had brought back off picket duty the previous day. Doyle had seen some enemy activity and had reported it to his senior officers but the report did not seem to stir any sense of urgency in them, as numerous such reports were being received almost every day. Private Hefferon's brother, James, was a trumpeter and servant to Lieutenant Viscount John Fitzgibbon.

Some men were sharing flasks of rum. Major John Halkett, second in command of the 4th Light Dragoons, had just come off sick leave to be with his men and he had not been issued with any rum. He asked a member of a group of officers, which included Lord Paget, if they could spare any. The two senior officers had not been on speaking terms for some time. However, Paget decided to ignore their differences under the circumstances and offered his flask, for which Halkett was thankful. Halkett had brought with him a small portable camera that had been made for him in London, but whether he managed to use it will never be known. Also in the gathering of 4th Light Dragoons officers was Lieutenant Henry Arthur Sparke, a son of the Reverend J.H. Sparke, the Canon of Ely.

Privates Robert Farquharson and Thomas Lovelock had been practically brought up together in the 4th Light Dragoons. Farquharson had asked his comrade if he had any 'grog' to spare, and while Lovelock was explaining that he had just given the last he had to the RSM, Farquharson noticed that his friend looked serious and depressed. On enquiring about his welfare Lovelock pointed out the guns being brought up by the enemy, and announced a melancholy foreboding: '... many of us will never get back to the lines again.' Some men in the ranks of the 4th were making last-minute adjustments to their accoutrements. Private Thomas Fletcher, 'a brave soldier and a splendid horseman', was helping his friend, Private James Herbert, to button up his straps.

The 8th Hussars were under the temporary command of Major Rodolph de Salis because Colonel Shewell was held up in his tent suffering from gout and sickness, probably caused by the deprivations and rigours of being on active service; this had prompted some of his men to call him 'the Old Woman'. Several other Hussars were laid up, including the disgruntled RSM Robert Harding, who had a nasty boil on his leg. However, having received news that his regiment might be going into action the Colonel pluckily returned to duty at once and to the satisfaction of his men he arrived to take charge. One man reportedly shouted out cheerfully from the ranks as he arrived: 'Well, I'm damned if it isn't the Colonel! What do you say to the "old woman" now?'

Among the other officers of the 8th Hussars was Captain George Lockwood, who was acting as ADC to Lord Cardigan. He was the 36-year-old son of the late William Joseph Lockwood of Dews Hall, a stately home near Lambourne in Essex. His father had fought with the Coldstream Guards under the Duke of Wellington at Talavera and Busaco in the Peninsular War; Captain Lockwood had only a month earlier been informed of his death. Another young officer was Augustus Frederick Webb, a Captain with the Death or Glory Boys. He was a Geordie from Westwick in Durham.

Lord Paget was enjoying a cigar and many men in the ranks of the 8th Hussars were also 'warming their noses'. However, Colonel Shewell was a strict disciplinarian and he disapproved of this and made his feelings known, making an example of one man in particular. Sergeant William Williams was just lighting his pipe when the commanding officer saw him and ordered his arrest, stating that he was disgracing the regiment by smoking in the face of the enemy. The sergeant tried to argue his corner by pointing out that the pipe was not yet lit, but he was disarmed and ordered to fall out. However, he was allowed to return to the ranks unarmed to be with his brother, Samuel, who was a Troop Sergeant-Major. Paget contemplated whether he should show a good example to his men but a good cigar was a rare commodity that day and it went with him into battle.

Cornet Hugh Montgomery was an Old Harrovian, whose father owned large estates in the north of Ireland. His cousin, Robert James Montgomery, had just taken part in the Charge of the Heavy Brigade. Lieutenant Percy Smith, 13th Light Dragoons, 'a cool-headed soldier', had lost part of his right hand in a gun accident before the war and had a protective iron guard made to slip over his wrist. In the dark that morning he could not find it in the tent and turned out without it. He was unable to use a weapon, so if there was any action he could only hope to encourage the men around him. These included Private William Wilson, 8th Hussars, who is believed to have been only 16 years old. Sergeant Richard Williams, 17th Lancers, was wearing a blood-stained bandage around his face to protect a painfully sore abscess on his nose. 'My visage was so fearsome that the Russians held their fire.'

One of the most colourful characters that day was 'a gruesome yet laughable fellow' named Private John Vahey, who was known in the 17th Lancers as 'Butcher Jack'. He was the regimental butcher who had been drinking that morning while he was working at the Commissariat depot at Balaclava slaughtering beasts. When he heard that there had been some action he decided to re-join his regiment. He was wearing a red cap, but he had no coat on and the sleeves of his blue shirt were turned up above his elbows. He was still wearing his white canvas smock with his trousers tucked into his boots, both being splattered in blood, and he was carrying a poleaxe. His face, arms and hands were also covered in blood. As he raced to join his unit he stopped near the body of a dead man of the Heavy Brigade to pick up a scabbard which he buckled around his waist and mounted a loose Heavies horse. He also acquired a sword. He came up between the two squadrons of the 1st Dragoons as they were moving forward in support of the Light Brigade. Colonel John Yorke looked round and said: 'Sergeant that man does not belong to my regiment, who is he?' Vahey answered, 'I belong to the 17th Lancers, sir.' Colonel Yorke replied, 'I admire your spirit my man, but you had better join your own regiment.' To which the butcher replied, 'All right, sir', and he galloped away. He then went to the 11th Hussars in the second line but he was sent away again. He eventually caught up with the 17th Lancers, where Lieutenant John Chadwick told him to join his own 2nd squadron. As he tried to do so he was refused admission because of his improper dress. The officer in command, presumably Captain Morris, was so impressed by his devotion that he shouted: 'Let the brave fellow in!' and he formed up on the right side of Private John Lees, demonstrating that he would be: 'darned if he was going to be left behind his regiment and lose the fun.'

Then came the sound of a horse's hoofs galloping with a rush towards them, and men began to raise themselves up in their stirrups and crane their necks to try to identify a lone horseman who approached from their left and rode up the gap between the 17th and 13th and called out to Captain Morris: 'Where is Lord Lucan?' Morris recognised the man as Captain Nolan and pointed towards Lord Lucan sitting on his horse in front of the two Brigades, at the same time asking: 'Are we going to charge?' Nolan was already off in the direction of the Brigade commander, but looking back over his shoulder with his eyes wide and filled with a look of great anticipation, he shouted: 'You will see! You will see!'

Captain Nolan had little respect for the Brigade commander and after reporting that the ground ahead was clear and there were none of the enemy in a position to ambush an advance, he thrust the note at him. Lucan opened it and on reading it a look of bewilderment came onto his face. Lucan did not have the extensive range of view that Lord Raglan had up on the ridge. He could see no significant enemy activity except in the distance at the far end of the valley, where the eight-gun Russian battery was situated. Nolan impatiently urged him to attack: 'Lord Raglan's orders are that the cavalry should attack immediately.'

Lucan retorted angrily, 'Attack, Sir! Attack what? What guns, sir?'

Nolan pointed vaguely eastward, and replied sharply, 'There, my Lord, is your enemy; there are your guns. It is your duty to take them!' He drew his sword 'with a flourish' and moved off to take up a position in front of the 17th Lancers, fully intending to participate in the action. Lord Lucan shrugged his shoulders. It would seem that he must order the Light Brigade to attack the Russian guns at the other end of the valley. There was a strange silence, broken only by the sound of the hooves of restless horses stamping on the ground and snorting, and the clatter of metal accoutrements, as Lord Lucan cantered over to Lord Cardigan: 'There you are, your Lordship, you've got to charge and take the guns!'

The brothers-in-law disliked each other; but on hearing the orders, Lord Cardigan maintained military courtesy by presenting his sabre in salute, remarking: 'Certainly, sir, but allow me to point out to you that the Russians have batteries in the valley to our front and on each side, and the ground is covered with riflepits!' Lord Lucan reminded Lord Cardigan that the order had come from Lord Raglan and they had no choice but to obey. Lord Cardigan had visibly paled at the contents of the note, but his coolness was commendable considering what he was being asked to do. He rode down the middle of the Brigade and on approaching his second in command he stated in what seemed like a tone of excitement: 'Lord George, we are ordered to make an attack to the front. You will take command of the second line, and I expect your best support.' He emphasised the point: 'Mind, your best support!' Considering the implication of the remark to be somewhat disrespectful, Lord Paget answered with equal emphasis: 'Of course, my Lord, you shall have ... my best support!'

Lord Cardigan then rode off to retake his place at the front of the Brigade. Remembering that he was the only boy in a family of eight siblings said: 'Well, here goes the last of the Brudenells.' Remaining erect and composed in his saddle he turned towards his men and brought his sabre down in salute, wheeled Ronald around to face the massive enemy force spread out all over the hills before him and in his firm, hoarse voice gave the order: 'The Brigade will advance. Walk. March, trot. First squadron of the 17th Lancers will direct!' He told his 'Death or Glory' orderly trumpeter, William Brittain, to sound the advance and led the Brigade forward, being about three horse-lengths ahead of them – surely realising he was virtually a sitting duck to the enemy gunners and sharpshooters.

3

MAGNIFICENT MADNESS

'For Christ's sake, men, come on!
Do you want to live forever?'

GUNNERY-SERGEANT DAN DALY, US MARINE CORPS

'Never was such a mad order given,' and troopers looked at each other in bewilderment and disbelief as they could see what a mistake was being made. Someone had blundered, but they had to obey orders even though they knew that many, if not all of them, would not be coming back. Private George Wootton, a baker from Worcester, 'an unsophisticated' man, who had shown a great deal of emotion at what he had witnessed at the Battle of the Alma, looked at Private Edward Woodham with concern on his face, and announced: 'Ted, old fellow, I know we shall charge!' Woodham raised himself up on his stirrups and after scanning the hills all around replied: 'Oh, nonsense, look at the strength in front of us. We're never going to charge there!' However, as the Brigade began to pick up pace Private Woodham turned back with a look of astonished realisation on his face and cried out: 'Yes, we're going to charge, and with a vengeance too!'

At the eastern end of the valley the Don Cossacks were busy preparing their field pieces ready to help to defend the ground their comrades had gained from the possibility of what they thought would be a strong British counter-attack. As they did so, their attention was brought to clouds of dust being stirred up by something moving in formation in the distance to the west. As eyes strained to see exactly what it was, it became clear that a comparatively small number of cavalry had come into view, moving steadily down a slope and into the valley. Russian officers were not concerned at first because they thought that such a small number of men would not be sent to attack such a massive force. They would not stand a chance. But looks of disbelief cossed many Muskovite faces when the Brigade began to pick up pace as they approached and it became obvious that these suicidal madmen were coming on and into the attack. Orders rang out with a sense of shock and urgency; and what was about to happen would be engraved in the minds of everyone who witnessed it for as long as they drew breath.

The Brigade made its way down the forward slope at a walk, and then broke into a trot as they rode over some churned-up land, moving on in a steady gallop as they got back onto firmer grassland. The 11th Hussars dropped back and Lord Paget guided his men at a slower pace than the rest until the correct distance of 200 yards between the lines was achieved. The finest cavalry on earth moved down the valley. The rigours of campaigning had left their mark on their magnificent uniforms but their rich colours still stood out against the dull Crimean terrain. At about 300 yards, flashes and clouds of smoke began to appear on the hills on each side and ear-splitting booms thundered dreadfully across the valley. There was the ceaseless crash of artillery as the Brigade rode into a shower of shot and shell from the Russian hardware that was situated to

The 13th Light Dragoons taking their place in line as the Light Brigade prepares to move off down the slope and into the valley ahead, where they rode into immortality.

the left on the Fedioukine Hills, to the right on the Causeway Heights, and from the front. The mouth of Hell had suddenly opened – and they were about to be led right into it.

Nolan beamed as the Brigade moved off. He believed that a cavalry action could not fail if delivered with speed but they had advanced quite a distance and were still being held at a steady trot. He became agitated at the slow progress and to the surprise of everyone near him he raised his sword in the air and spurred his horse forward. Realising that his eagerness had got the better of him, Captain Morris shouted a warning to him: 'That won't do, Nolan. We've a long way to go and must be steady!' Nolan did not respond and he galloped across the advancing line from left to right, with his sword waving in the air. Private George Badger was riding in the front rank of the 13th Light Dragoons, and Nolan barged into him and knocked him to one side as he crossed the front of the line. Still waving his sabre in the air he was seen to turn and shout something, but his words became lost in the din of battle. As he turned to the front again a shell from a northerly direction burst close to him, from which a piece of jagged metal shot out at him, shattered his rib-cage, ripped into his chest and tore it apart. With a look of agony he gave out a terrible shriek as his sword dropped from his hand, although his arm remained erect for a while. He thrust his twitching bridle hand against his chest, which was becoming more and more blood-soaked with every second. This spooked his horse and caused it to rear up and he slumped from the charger with his leg trapped in the stirrups. The horse bolted and he was dragged along for a distance before it suddenly stopped and remained standing over its master's lifeless body as the rest of the Brigade rode past.

Lord Cardigan, rigidly facing ahead, led his men forward through the heavy, acrid smoke and the dust kicked up by their horses' hooves. They began to lose sight of each other as it encircled them like fog. There was the continuous rattle of rifles, which sent musket balls whining through the air around them and men gave sighs of relief as they felt the slipstream of missiles going past and not hitting them this time; although they were aware that some of their comrades behind them would not be so fortunate. The roar of cannon was deafening and shells ripped up the ground all around them. The shells sent men and horses sprawling over each other, or shattered them to pieces. Limbs were torn from bodies and heads blown from shoulders as shells exploded above and around them, spattering men with blood and guts, and there was a horrible thud and splashing sound as groups of troopers were blasted out of existence. Men struggled to free themselves from beneath their fallen horses, or writhed in agony among the carnage left behind as the wave of British cavalry raced forward. As the shocked onlookers began to realise Lord Cardigan's objective, General Pierre Bosquet of the French army remarked: 'C'est magnifique, mais ce n'est pas la guerre: c'est de la folie.' (It is magnificent, but it is not war: it is madness).

The Heavy Brigade was ordered to advance and prepare to go in support of the Light Brigade. As they wheeled to the right and came around the ridge of the Causeway into the north valley, they could hardly believe the enormous task before them. They could just see through the dust and smoke the outline of the Light Brigade galloping towards the Russian lines. As they moved forward building up their pace as they did so, they came into direct line of fire, and men and horses were knocked over by shot and shell, which also ploughed up the ground all around them. One shell dropped into the middle of a group of 5th Dragoon Guards and six horses and their troopers were scattered by the sheer force of the blast, which left them in a straggling mass. Three brothers were involved in this incident. 'Little Trumpeter Stacey was severely

As men of the Light Brigade thundered into the mouth of hell with bullets whizzing about their heads like hail and cannon balls bouncing at them and exploding all around, they were also hampered by frenzied loose horses with empty saddles on their backs.

wounded, and a young lad named Arlett had his arm blown off by a cannon shot.'
A musket ball caught Lieutenant-Colonel Yorke on the left shin-bone and smashed it.
He was forced to fall out and rode down to the harbour feeling sick and delirious with
pain, the limb swinging about loosely for all to see. As the 1st Division of infantry
began to arrive the Heavies retired out of range of the enemy's relentless barrages.

Private Wightman remembered the position of each man near him. Private John
Lees was to his left, Private Peter Marsh was to his right; next beyond him was Private
Thomas Dudley. The Light Brigade had not yet increased their pace to a gallop when a
cannon shell smashed into the body of Private Lees and the explosion tore him apart.
As he breathed his last he reached out and plucked Private Wightman's arm. With a
look on his face suggesting he knew his fate he quietly said: 'Domino! chum', as what
was left of him sank from the saddle and slithered to the floor. Private Wightman
recalled: 'His old grey mare kept along side me for some distance, tearing out and
treading on her entrails as she galloped, till at length she dropped with a strange
shriek.'

The Brigade began to take echelon shape as the 11th Hussars veered to their left
and moved closer to the Fedioukine Hills, where they soon began to suffer the full
force of enemy fire from that side of the valley. Trumpeter Brittain was blown from
his horse and mortally wounded, and the 11th Hussars began to lose men fast as
round shot slammed into them from all directions. Private Wootton was eager to get
at the enemy. He galloped forward out of the line and was struck by a missile and
killed instantly. Private David Ward, a slubber from Leeds, was struck by a direct hit
in the chest which smashed him out of his saddle, and a cannon ball took off Private

'The Death or Glory Boys' in the front line of the attack were almost upon the guns when a
cannonade from almost all the guns at once blew great gaps in their line.

Richard Albert Young's arm, showering TSM Loy Smith's helmet and jacket with bits of his flesh. Private George Turner attempted to raise his sword in the air before he realised that a shell had ripped his right arm off at the socket. Both men turned to their sergeant for guidance, and he simply told them to turn back and get to the rear for medical attention as fast as they could. The officers of the 11th Hussars fared no better, as a shell burst overhead and the shrapnel struck Lieutenant George Houghton in the forehead and he went down with a crash mortally wounded and Lieutenant Harington Trevelyan fell out when he was hit.

A square of infantry had formed up on the side of the hill to their left and gave them a volley in flank. The air hissed as the shower of bullets passed through them and men were killed or wounded. There were some near misses too, as a bullet passed through the back of Private William Humphries' neck and just missed his spinal cord, while a slug passed across the front of Sergeant-Major Smith's body and cut and blackened the lace on the left hand cuff of his tunic. RSM George Bull, and Trumpeters John Keates and William Smith had their horses shot from under them.

Seeing the havoc the Russians were causing to the Brits from the left flank on the Fedioukine Heights, the 4th Chasseurs d'Afrique were brought into action, led by Colonel Champeron and Major Abdelal. Advancing in two lines, although using their tactical open formation, four squadrons charged hell for leather along the escarpment at the Russian cannon and the infantry sharpshooters hidden in rifle pits. With the loss of fewer than 40 casualties they succeeded in silencing the guns and putting the enemy to flight. The action was well executed and precise, preventing the Russians in this area from causing further casualties to the Light Brigade and to the Heavy Brigade, who were moving forward in support. The action also did good service for the Light Brigade as they returned over the same area a short time later.

Lord Paget was looking left and right as he led his men onward, now and again yelling out the order: 'Steady men, steady!' The 4th Light Dragoons did not check and continued on at speed, and therefore they and the 8th Hussars eventually advanced separately and the Brigade took even more of an echelon shape as the pace increased. Captain Thomas Hutton, 4th Light Dragoons, winced and cried out as he received a slug in the right thigh. He reported this to his squadron leader, Captain Alexander Low. On asking what he should do, Captain Low suggested: 'If you can sit on your horse you had better come with us, there's no use going back now, you'll only be killed.' In the ranks Private Lovelock was killed and Private Herbert noticed that Private Fletcher was dropping back and losing the line. Herbert had just shouted: 'Keep up, Tom!' when a bullet fizzed by and grazed him, followed by a thud as it hit his comrade in the back of his head and killed him. Private William Pearson's horse stumbled over one that had fallen before it and he crashed to the ground. Still dazed, he managed to grab hold of the stirrups of a riderless horse and dragged himself up into the saddle. He had an epaulette shot from his shoulder and received a wound to the forehead.

Private William Bird, 8th Hussars, described feeling '...a sort of sensation of madness', as the 8th Hussars veered to the right as they approached the guns in order to take the Russian flank. This brought them closer to the fire from the Causeway and they were peppered with musket balls. Lieutenant Edward Seager was riding in front of the centre of the regiment when his mare 'Malta' got a slug through her neck just above the windpipe, but she stayed on her feet and they pushed bravely on. Lieutenant Fitzgibbon jerked back fiercely as he was hit in the chest by two bullets almost simultaneously. He lost his grip on his sabre, which was strapped to his arm, and clasping his hands to his chest he groaned loudly: 'Oh, my God, my God, I am shot!' Some men slowed down with the intention of offering assistance but the officer cried out: 'Go on, go on', before he slumped lifeless from his horse. Privates Hefferon and Lennon were still eating the biscuits and meat that Private Doyle had given them, when Hefferon was hit by a shell which exploded and blew the top half of his body into the air, leaving his hips and legs in the saddle. As Jemmy was chasing at the hooves of Private Lennon's charger and yapping at the cannon balls as they bounded by, his master was struck in the side of the head by a round shot which took most of it away. As his lifeless body lay on the ground the loyal dog pranced around it barking for him to get up, and as it did so was pelted in the neck by splinters of shell and began to yowl in pain. Everyone riding close to these men was splattered by their remains.

The order was yelled out by Hussar and Light Dragoon officers for their men to draw swords, and lances came down. The front line of the brigade was so close to the Russian battery that the thundering noise of the cannon blasts rang through the heads of the men. In a last desperate effort to try to stop the attack the Don Cossacks loaded their field pieces with double-shot of shell and case and a murderous fusillade from most of the guns at once smashed into the front line of horsemen, blasting sections of the 13th Light Dragoons and 17th Lancers into oblivion. A shell burst under Captain Oldham's horse, blew its hind legs off and knocked over two or three other horses. The officer himself was not hit but he was thrown violently from his charger. The next moment he threw up his hands as he was almost immediately hit by a musket-ball and fell. Private Badger was wounded in the side by a metal fragment and knocked senseless when his horse was brought down; on recovering consciousness he saw Captain Oldham lying nearby. The officer called him over and asked him to take a watch and purse from him; but as Badger moved towards him another ball struck his commander and he fell back dead, still clutching the personal items he was holding out. Seeing Cossacks advancing, Badger caught the stirrup of a loose horse but he was unable to run due to his wound and he had to let it go. As the Cossacks stopped by the dead officer to search him for plunder he was able to make his escape.

Of the other men of the 13th Light Dragoons who were hit by this barrage, Private John Brooks was wounded as his horse was blown apart by a shell and Corporal Edward W Aubrey Smith was struck full in the face, smashing his head to pieces. His mutilated body fell to the earth and his horse galloped on. Another shell struck the horse of Private Albert Mitchell, carrying away the shoulder and part of the chest, horse and rider fell in a heap. Fortunately, he was shielded by his horse's carcass when the shell exploded a few yards off. On recovering from the shock he found that his left leg was trapped beneath the body of the heavy beast, and as he tried to free himself he heard the second line of 4th Light Dragoons come galloping towards him, and he fully expected to be trampled to death. He called out, 'For God's sake, don't ride over me.' He eventually succeeded in freeing himself, being unhurt apart from his crushed leg.

The 17th Lancers suffered just as terribly from this cannonade. Captain Robert White was thinking that they would be better off to get into the guns and out of the fire – the lesser of two evils – when Captain Winter's E Troop of the 2nd squadron was swept away as they took the full force of the gun blasts. Captain Winter was shot to pieces and after his body had fallen to the ground his frenzied horse, although wounded by grapeshot, careered all the way back to the British lines. Lancer Private Dudley was shocked by the amount of carnage he witnessed and called out: 'What a bloody hole that shell has made.' Private Peter Marsh yelled back sternly: 'Hold your foul-mouthed tongue from swearing like a blackguard when you may be knocked into eternity next minute!' Sergeant Edward Talbot had his head blown off his shoulders and his body remained in the saddle riding headless for a considerable distance, still clutching the reins and holding onto his lance. A shell pierced the chest of the horse of Private Robert Evans, which burst inside the animal and tore it open from the shoulders to the hindquarters. As they hit the ground the horse rolled over on top of him and he was being crushed by the weight of the animal. He received terrible contusions to his left leg as the horse writhed in agony. Fortunately, a man of his troop and two Lancers released him, but his leg went under the knife later. Private Charles Allured was shot in the temple and killed. A little further on, Lieutenant Harington Trevalyan was shot in the left calf, but with Sergeant Bond's encouragement he kept going under fire and thereby had the protection of a group of his own soldiers rather than falling out with the risk of being picked off by enemy sharpshooters.

Now began the most violent man-to-man fighting of the whole affair as the Light Brigade plunged headlong in at the enemy cannon. On realising that the British were not going to be stopped, panic-stricken Russian drivers tried desperately to limber-up the guns while being hacked and slashed at mercilessly as they tried to get away. The gunners tried to defend their field pieces by fending off the attackers with their rammers, but flashing British sabres cut many of them down. Others scurried under their guns to try to escape the fearsome attackers, only to be hunted out and slashed and stabbed to death.

Butcher Jack survived the massive cannonade that had blasted away many of his comrades. He smashed his way into the guns and with one blow of his axe he bludgeoned the head of a gunner just as he was about to light a fuse. Pushing on, he came upon a Russian officer who was trying to rally an artillery detachment at the rear, and with one blow he cut the man down. His horse was shot and he lay insensible beneath it. He was eventually released, and – now sober – he set off back up the valley.

Corporal Penn had also survived on his mount, Nancy, and raced at the guns. He brought his lance down and aiming the point at a Cossack gunner he skewered the man through the body. He could not pull the weapon out and he had to let go of it. Beyond the guns he saw a Russian Hussar officer and spurred his horse at the man, who wheeled his horse about and galloped off. Penn gave chase, and as he came alongside the Russian he slashed the man across the neck and he slumped from the horse. Penn dismounted and approached the enemy officer's lifeless, almost headless body. He grabbed his pouch, took a large knife which he thrust into his own belt, and picked up his sword. Nancy had been hit in the shoulder by a musket ball, but he re-mounted and looking around, he saw Privates Edward Holland and Samuel Hunscott of his regiment, and Charles Powell of the 11th Hussars, surrounded by Cossack horsemen and in great peril, so digging his spurs in he raced forward to offer help. Charging into the middle of the fight he thrashed his sabre at the Cossacks to keep them back and used another old cavalry trick, cutting at the reins of their chargers. He managed to surprise and dismount at least three of the enemy in this way.

Sergeant Thomas George John Johnson, 13th Light Dragoons, passed through the guns and on approaching the enemy's cavalry at the rear of the battery, he and Private John Keeley found themselves within a few yards of Lord Cardigan, who was surrounded by and engaged in defending himself against four or five Cossack Lancers. They attempted to go to Cardigan's assistance, but they had not gone far when their horses were shot from under them. He then saw Lord Cardigan disengage himself from the Cossacks and ride away apparently unhurt, although one of the Cossacks attempted a right rear point at him with his lance. (Cardigan would return with a couple of wounds but is not certain if the Cossack actually struck home.)

The 8th Hussars attacked the right flank of the battery. Private John Doyle on his horse, Hickabod, saw an enemy officer dash into the centre of the melee at the rear of the guns, where he wounded a number of men of the 8th Hussars, slicing the skin off the side of the head of Private (Richard or George) Kennedy. As the officer turned to attack him, Doyle presented his sword and parried his blade with a 'right-rear point'. As the retreat sounded the same officer heard it and endeavoured to get in front of Doyle to stop him from getting away. However, Private Doyle had the measure of him and met him right hand to right hand. The officer made a stab at him but Doyle was too quick for him. After smashing the Russian's weapon out of the way he drove his sword through his mouth, and the horribly wounded officer rode off. The young trooper was twisting and turning like an eel in the saddle, parrying the enemy's points and returning his own, and he wounded many more men. Hickabod received a bullet through the nose that caused him to lose a great deal of blood – every time he threw his head back the blood spurted over his rider. Doyle had the first finger of his bridle

Having seen many of their comrades blown out of existence, the Lancers who survived were immediately in the thick of the fighting, slashing left and right and stabbing their lances. There was no escape for the enemy and they were mercilessly cut to pieces.

hand split in five places and a piece cut out of his thumb. Coming out of the action at the guns he was hit by the point of a lance in the forehead.

The 8th Hussars halted about 400 yards beyond the guns, where they formed up and waited about five minutes for orders; surely one of the most unearthly pauses in any military action in history. They were joined by a few others, chiefly from the 17th Lancers, making in all about 70 men. As they did so Corporal William Taylor's charger, spooked with all the noise and destruction around it, became so wild he lost control of the animal. It bolted ahead and into the midst of the Russian cavalry beyond the guns, where the corporal was wounded and taken prisoner. At about the same time a sergeant noticed that his fellow NCO, Sergeant Edward Reilly, was not in his right place in the line and warned him of this. When no response came he turned towards Reilly and an eerie sight met his eyes. His fellow sergeant's lifeless body was sat upright, motionless in the saddle with his eyes fixed and staring blankly out of his rigid, pale face.

As the 11th Hussars passed by the left flank of the Russian gun battery, Sergeant Richard Brown was on the artillerymen and all over them, until a 24-pounder fired

Mad-eyed 11th Hussars smash headlong into the panic-stricken Don Cossack gunners and drivers, slashing at them with their sabres.

from close range took his horse's foreleg clean off and they crashed to earth. Getting to his feet, he slashed at one gunner, cut another's arm off as he raised his rammer at him, and lifted the scalp off another man's head. Then two mounted Cossacks attacked him and he exchanged slashing blades with them in a frantic fury until he got inside one man's lance and cut half way through his body. He fell, and as the other Cossack misjudged a charge the sergeant parried his thrust and cut the Russian's throat with a back-handed slash.

Sergeant Robert Davis, 11th Hussars, saw one of the end guns limbered up and ready to be taken away. He called to Private John Bambrick, who was riding next to him, to assist him in an effort to capture the field piece. Two enemy Lancers rode up to defend the gun. He cut one down but the other presented his carbine and shot Davis's horse. They tumbled to the floor and as he lay on the ground he received a lance wound in the thigh. His assailant then rode off. Davis managed to catch a loose horse on which he returned to his regiment. Bambrick's horse was also shot.

While covering the rear of the regiment, TSM Loy Smith saw three panic-stricken drivers desperately trying to control a team of six horses to take away a large brass gun. He decided to try to stop them and called out to three men who were near him to join him in the task. He rode off towards the gun but at the point of attack he realised that the three men had not come with him; to add to the impossibility of the task a Russian Hussar officer and three Cossacks were on their way towards him to prevent the gun's capture. TSM Smith reined in and galloped towards them with the apparent intention of taking all four of them on single-handedly. As usual, this caused the enemy to hesitate and he was able to avoid the unequal confrontation and re-join his regiment.

The 4th Light Dragoons then came in and engaged the artillerymen. As they did so Private Parkes noticed that Lord Paget's sword was still in his scabbard. 'Come on, my Lord', he shouted to his leader, 'It is time you were drawing your sword – we are on top of the guns!' His Lordship drew the weapon at once, and almost immediately thrust it through the neck of a gunner. A desperate hand-to-hand struggle ensued.

Captain Low was a very powerful, muscular man who was handy with his sword, and was described as 'the best cavalry officer out there'. He was fighting like a man possessed, and in a wild frenzy he was cutting and slashing at anything that moved. He killed thirteen gunners and when three cavalrymen got in his way he quickly pulled out his revolver and shot the first two and ran the third one through with the point of his sabre. 'Much gore besmeared him' as he finished his gruesome task. He assembled a troop of his men and attempted to capture a Russian gun.

Private Parkes needed to stay close to both Lord Paget and Trumpeter Hugh Crawford, who relayed the Commanding Officer's orders to the troops. However, Parkes' horse was shot from under him and he became detached from them. He shouted anxiously: 'Where's my chief? Who's seen the Colonel?' Fortunately the honourable member for Beaumaris was not too far away and his Lordship replied:

A Russian's-eye-view of a trooper of the 4th Light Dragoons as he gallops into action with the second line of the Brigade, glaring savagely and swirling his sabre in the air ready to slash at anyone who got near him or that he could hunt down.

'Here I am, my boy, I'm all right.' Reassured by this, Parkes became embroiled in fierce hand-to-hand combat and he was surrounded by Russians. He was fighting with great determination and was about to attack a Russian when one of his officers called out: 'Spare him Sam!' Parkes ignored this strange request and finished off the Russian with his sabre.

Other 4th Light Dragoons men set about the enemy gunners and the drivers. No hammers had been issued to the Light Brigade, but those who had acquired spikes knocked them in with the hilt of their sabres or simply gripped their hands as tight as they could around the spike and tried to force it in. Lieutenant Hedworth Joliffe and Sergeant Frederick Short did good work. The officer shot down several gunners who were sitting at their guns while the latter dealt with at least six drivers and their horses. Private Dennis Connor tried to cut the traces of a gun with his pocket knife as Cornet George Hunt, Sergeant John Howes and Private Robert Ferguson dismounted and attempted to harness the cannon to get it away. Connor found that the traces had been strengthened with steel chains inside the leather and could not be cut, so they were forced to abandon their work. Lord Paget ordered them to remount, and Howes had to do it on a 'brute of a horse'. While he was making his way back up the valley, Sergeant Howes received a slight cut on the side of his head after an encounter with a Russian Hussar. Many of the gunners were standing in groups firing their rifles and the Brits cut at them as they went rushing by. As Private Joseph Grigg reached the rear of the guns a mounted driver slashed him across the eyes with a whip and almost blinded him. Still trying to blink away the blurred vision, Grigg made a sword cut across the lower part of the face of his assailant the blade grating against the teeth. Grigg made a second cut at him to finish him off as he fell from his horse. He slashed a second driver across the back of his neck and gave him a second cut too as he collapsed and slumped to the ground.

At this point the 11th Hussars were fighting in the area between the left flank of the guns and the eastern end of the Fedioukine Hills, advancing round a bend to the left which took them down the track leading to the Traktir Bridge and the Tchernaya River. The 8th Hussars were engaged with the enemy between the right flank of the guns and the eastern end of the Causeway Heights and in the area beyond the battery on that side of the valley. The 4th Light Dragoons were mainly embroiled in combat amongst the guns, while remnants of the 13th Light Dragoons and the 17th Lancers were joining other units as best they could, or had already started their journey back up the valley. Colonel Douglas saw Lord Paget and approached him saying: 'What are we to do now, Lord Paget?' and Paget replied: 'Where is Lord Cardigan?' Then he galloped back towards the guns.

Colonel Douglas then led forward his surviving unit of about 80 men, including one man of the 13th Light Dragoons and a 17th Lancer. They soon found themselves face-to-face with the same cavalry that had been put in reverse by the Heavy Brigade. Heavily outnumbered, but with fired-up blood, Colonel Douglas yelled the order: 'Give them another charge, men! Hoorah!' The Hussars raised their sabres above their heads and swirled them around, what must have been a dramatic, terrifying sight, then charged pell mell at the edgy enemy horsemen. Having already witnessed numerous extraordinary examples of British pluck, and seeing this small unit of fearless maniacs galloping towards them, the mass of enemy horsemen wheeled about and fell back. The British attacked those who were hesitant and cut them down without mercy and yelled mocking remarks after the main body as they raced on in pursuit.

The Russians were so disorganised and panic-stricken that several men fell over the sides of the Traktir Bridge and plummeted into the water as they jostled to get across it. The rest galloped on towards a moderately steep hill beyond. As the Russians ascended the hill they stopped suddenly and with their backs to the British they looked over their shoulders like 'a vast assemblage in the gallery of a theatre' looking at the stage. They turned and the two forces were standing facing each other just a few horse lengths apart. There was an unbearably tense moment of stillness and silence, as men on both sides eyed each other up and down the ranks. Some glared with the utmost contempt, some snarled and grimaced with the intention of intimidating the men directly in front of them, while others looked ill at ease and unsure what to do next.

This deathly silence was broken by Russian officers who yelled out orders and urged their horses forward into action, racing at the front ranks of the 11th and trying to break through. However, their men hesitated and faltered yet again, as the 11th Hussars showed a firm front by closing together and presenting their sabres in a defensive stance, managing to hold the enemy back for several minutes. The Russian officers then presented their pistols and fired, while Cossacks circled around the flanks and attacked the men at the rear of the unit. The 11th Hussars were now in an almost hopeless situation and it seemed certain that they would soon be overwhelmed and killed to a man.

Three squadrons of Russian Lancers had ridden down from the hillside and were blocking their retreat, recognisable to some of the men as the enemy because of the green and white pennons hanging from their lance heads. Colonel Douglas exclaimed: 'They're the 17th, let us rally on them!' At that moment Lieutenant Roger Palmer rode up and said, 'I beg your pardon, Colonel. That is not the 17th, that is the enemy.' Douglas replied: 'Then fight for your lives, men! We must only retire and go through them.' He yelled the order: 'Threes about!' and 'Charge!' Sections of British horsemen were brought into formation, wheeled about and turned their backs on the Hussars they had just pursued and galloped at the Lancers. As they did so, the Hussars regained some of their nerve and moved forward after them, menacing them from behind.

Several horses began to slow down with fatigue and their riders could not keep up with the unit, among them Sergeant William Bentley and Private Robert Levett, both Yorkshiremen. Cossacks began to move in on the stragglers and Sergeant Bentley was attacked from behind. As he tried to fend off his attackers a bullet grazed his calf, and a lance prod in the neck knocked him off his horse. He clambered to his feet and retaliated by slashing an enemy officer across the face with his sword. Private Levett was also being attacked and both men looked lost.

Lieutenant Alexander Dunn saw their plight and dropped back from the main body of men to offer assistance. The tall, Canadian-born officer had given his regimental sword away and had acquired one in England that was much longer than regulation. He charged at the enemy and smashed into them wielding his powerful sabre, violently hacking and slashing at them on his frenzied charger. A thrust to the body knocked a Cossack off his horse and two others followed. As a fourth Russian came near he raised the heavy sword above his head and brought it down with such force that it split the man's skull and almost cleaved him in half. Turning his attention to Private Levett, who was being attacked by a lancer, he charged at the man and with one stroke of his sabre he severed his neck and almost cut his head off. Levett had already been mortally wounded.

They were being driven towards the Lancers, who had started slowly to advance; but suddenly they halted and swung into line, allowing the British to gallop along their front, the men on the right parrying lance thrusts with their swords as they passed. Once again, the Russians' nerve failed and the Hussars broke through them. Further injuries were sustained nevertheless, such as that to Private John Smith Parkinson, who received a lance prod in the back of his neck, which did not bother him at the time. He then had his mount shot from under him and he had to catch a stray horse. His left leg was lacerated by a piece of sharp metal when a shell burst near to him, and in all he was wounded in three places. His left boot was ruined and he had to tie his foot up with a piece of old sacking. Private James Elder, who had been Sergeant Bond's servant that morning, was shot from his horse and as he staggered to get to his feet three pursuing Russians jabbed their lances at him and his body was pierced at least three times. Sergeant Bond received a sword thrust in his arm as he attempted to assist. He captured a loose horse on the return and gave it to Robert Briggs, 11th Hussars, which almost certainly saved his life. Bond's horse was badly wounded and would die after the action.

Private Robert Martin had his right arm shattered and he gathered up the now-useless limb as well as he could and laid it across his knees. The order to retire was given. A Cossack close to them levelled his pistol and fired at Martin and Private James Glanister. The bullet passed close by Martin's face and struck Glanister, shattering his lower jaw and causing him to fall forward on his cloak, which was rolled up in front of him. The Cossack bolted at once, and Private Martin had the presence of mind to grasp the reins of his horse and place them in his mouth, at the same time seizing those of Glanister's horse and turning it into the ranks. Glanister was unarmed as he had broken his sword off short at the hilt when striking a Russian on the top of his helmet while he was fighting at the guns. The two wounded men galloped back with the remnant of the regiment and they were making good progress when Martin began to feel faint from loss of blood. He urged his horse on as best he could to get him out of the range of fire, but a bullet struck his ammunition pouch. On arriving back at the British lines he was held up by an officer as he was given some rum, which had brought him to his senses. He was assisted off his horse and placed on a stretcher to be carried to the rear.

4

'EVERY MAN FOR HIMSELF!'

'Well, you have to be alive to feel sick!'

SIR STANLEY BAKER IN *ZULU!*

Back at the guns Lord Paget and the other officers saw that the enemy cavalry were re-forming, so the call to rally was sounded. Some troopers managed to locate each other amid the gun-smoke and got together in groups, but it was every man for himself as they started to run the gauntlet back to the British lines. As the British moved off, Russian artillerymen returned to their cannon and riflemen sent volleys up the valley, bringing down horses and men. They did not distinguish between friend and foe and many Russians were killed by shot from their own cannon. Lord Paget turned to Low and said: 'Low, we are in a terrible scrape. What the devil shall we do? Has anyone seen Lord Cardigan?' Low had indeed seen Lord Cardigan, 'riding back as fast as he could.' The order reportedly rang out: '4th Light Dragoons to the assistance of the 11th Hussars', and Cornet Fiennes Martin ordered his troop to respond. However, many of them were engaged in fighting with Cossack artillerymen and could not respond to the order.

Captain Hutton was shot through his other thigh but remained on his horse. Colonel Paget overtook him, saw that he was hurt and faint and passed him his rum flask. Hutton thanked him and said 'I have been wounded Colonel, would you have any objection to me going to the Doctor when I get in?' His horse had eleven wounds and would have to be destroyed.

On his return up the valley, Private Parkes came upon Trumpeter Crawford, whose horse had collapsed with exhaustion. Crawford was not badly injured by the fall but he was unarmed and two mounted Cossacks were moving in on him. Private Parkes, with complete disregard for his own safety, ran to Crawford's aid and placed himself between his comrade and the enemy. He raised his sword in a defensive position as he helped the trumpeter to his feet and supported him on one arm. He fended off the Cossacks with his sword and they were eventually driven away.

As the two men moved cautiously up the valley, trying to keep to areas that were thick with smoke to shield them from the view of marauding Russian horsemen, they came upon Major John Halkett collapsed on the ground. Halkett was second in command of their regiment. He had been on the sick list but had requested permission to return to duty. A shell had hit him full in the chest during the advance and he was covered in blood. He knew himself that he had no hope of survival. A unit of the 4th led by Captain Lowe had ridden by earlier and he called out to them: 'Take my money for the married women at home.' His wife had sewn some money into his belt. This was a gallant request, but prompted by the severity of his fellow officer's wounds and seeing Cossacks getting dangerously close, Lowe took the decision to ride on and try to save his surviving men.

Major Halkett immediately ordered his men to leave him and try to save themselves; but ignoring an order for the second time that day, and having been joined by Private John Edden, a fellow native of Tamworth in Staffordshire, Private Parkes asked him to lift the officer onto his back and they stumbled on as best they could. They had not gone far when six Cossacks appeared from out of the gloom, and knowing the burden was too much, the Major ordered Parkes to put him down and try to get away. This time the gallant trooper did as he was told and gently laid his officer down on the ground. The Major told them to take his money belt and with the intention of defending himself to the last, he asked them to put a sabre in his hand before they left.

Crawford could only make slow progress and as the enemy came nearer, Parkes once again placed himself before the oncoming horsemen, cutting and thrusting at them with his sword in a desperate attempt to keep them beyond striking distance. A Russian officer then came up and shouted in English: 'If you will give yourselves up you shall not be harmed.' The trooper refused. A Cossack then shot him in his right arm causing him to drop his weapon. They all attempted to run away but only Edden managed to escape. Suspecting that they may be treated badly by the Russians, Parkes requested the protection of the officer. As they were being escorted towards the enemy lines they came upon the body of Major Halkett, stripped of everything but his jacket.

Private Farquharson was confronted by a gunner. His horse was hit by a bullet and fell to the ground and as Farquharson struggled to get to his feet the gunner made a slash at him, which missed the mark and came down on the breast of the already wounded horse and caused a deep gash. While the Cossack was off-guard, Private Farquharson thrust the point of his sword through his head and killed him. As he made his way back he had become lost among the clouds of dense smoke; a man of his regiment with a badly injured arm rode up. Farquharson tore a strip from his overalls and tied it around the man's upper arm to stop the bleeding. He eventually mounted a stray horse belonging to the 17th Lancers which had tagged on to the back of the 11th Hussars as they fought their way back. As he returned a cannon ball came bounding towards him, hit his mount in the head and killed it. He fell with it to the ground. He was quickly surrounded by a party of Cossacks and taken prisoner.

Troop Sergeant-Major Denis O'Hara rallied about 15 of his Lancers and they were skirmishing and attacking at random. The Lancers eventually split up as TSM O'Hara took one small party and Colonel George Mayow, a member of the Brigade Staff, led the remainder against a body of Russian horsemen about 500 paces to the rear of the guns. They forced the Russians back. Colonel Mayow was confronted by a stocky Russian cavalry officer. He 'very cleverly' tipped off his shako with the point of his sword and then 'laid his head right open with the old cut seven'. They then joined a squadron of 8th Hussars and Colonel Shewell took command of the body of about 70 men.

As they pushed on along the valley, Lieutenant Seager rode up and informed them that a body of Polish Lancers, three ranks deep and with lances levelled to receive them, had emerged from the hills to their right and was blocking their escape route. Colonel Douglas consulted with his officers and it was decided that they had no option but to attack and try to break through. He gave the order: 'Right about wheel.' The unit came about as if on parade to face the enemy and show their determination to fight. Shewell, and Lieutenant-Colonel de Salis led the way, while Lieutenant Seager took charge of the 8th Hussars men. They broke into a charge, which visibly unnerved the enemy Lancers and some of them fled as they approached. The remainder waited to receive the attack; but they were so surprised at the steadiness of the British horsemen that they offered little resistance and the Light Brigade broke through them. Lieutenant Seager and his mount, Moses, parried the first enemy lance prod made at him and cut the next man he engaged over the head. As he was recovering his sword, a third man made a tremendous point at his body, which he just had time to receive on the hilt of his sword. The point got through the bow, knocked the skin off the knuckles of his second finger, and came out at the other side. The Russian considered he had done enough and galloped away as fast as he could.

These men then began to split up as this seemed to offer the greatest chance of survival. Many scattered to the left to get out of reach of the tremendous rifle fire being aimed at them, the shells bursting over them with an awful crash. A large body of enemy Lancers were approaching from the left to try to cut them off. Lieutenant Seager and his men spurred their horses on and sometimes walking, sometimes galloping, they got out of reach of the fire and the immediate peril.

Sergeant John Berryman, 17th Lancers, was near the guns when a round shot broke his mare's hind leg, causing him to stop immediately. He dismounted, and realised that he had received what he considered to be only a slight wound in the leg. He was considering whether to shoot his horse, when one of his officers, Captain Augustus Webb, came up to him. The Captain was still mounted but his right shin bone had been shattered and he had a gaping wound. Under the circumstances they decided that they should both try to get back up the valley. Sergeant Berryman eventually caught a loose horse, but almost at once an enemy missile hit the animal, driving the breastplate into its chest and it fell. He continued on foot, at one point running between squadrons of the 11th Hussars. In the confusion, he came across Captain Webb again, who was still mounted but in such agony from his wound that he could ride no farther. Sergeant Berryman got Lieutenant George Smith of his regiment to hold the horse steady at its head while he assisted Captain Webb off the animal and onto the ground. Lieutenant Smith then went off to look for something they could use as a stretcher. As he was waiting for assistance, Sergeant Berryman saw six Lancers all grouped together exchanging stories of their own individual actions and how they had escaped. The Sergeant spotted that the Russians had re-manned the guns. Reacting quickly to the danger he called out a warning, but before the men could respond, a shell dropped amongst them, and they were gone.

He was eventually joined by Sergeant John Farrell, 17th Lancers, and Corporal Joseph Malone, 13th Light Dragoons. Corporal Malone had been riding with Captain Arthur Tremayne's E Troop when his horse was shot from under him and he was trapped under the body of the dead animal until Corporal James Nunnerley, 17th Lancers, dragged the horse off him and set him free. He was continuing back to the British lines on foot when he came upon Sergeants Berryman and Farrell trying to assist their mortally wounded officer. Between them they made a 'king's chair' with their hands and tried to support his shattered leg. Private James Lamb, 13th Light Dragoons, met them near number 3 redoubt. Lamb's horse had been shot from under him during the advance, and although he had been thrown clear of the animal he had injured his leg. Captain Webb was feebly asking for water but Private Lamb's water bottle had been shot through, so he searched among the dead bodies all around them and found a 'calabash' half-full with water strapped to a dead trooper's saddle. On his way back to his comrades he took a drink himself before handing it to the officer to quench his thirst. As they carried the officer the 200 or so yards back to the British lines, Private Lamb limped along with them ready to offer any assistance if they needed it. As they got back the celebrated French General Morris met them and said to Berryman: 'Ah! And you, Sergeant, if you were in the French service I would make you an officer on the spot.' Captain Webb had his leg amputated, 'partially under the influence of chloroform', and died at Scutari Hospital.

As Lieutenant Dunn and Sergeant Bentley were making their way up the valley on foot, the officer saw an enemy trooper with his carbine aimed at Lieutenant

The 11th Hussars were originally mounted on white horses. Their elaborately decorated uniforms were blue with crimson busby bag head dress. The overalls (trousers) were crimson, a unique distinction authorised by Queen Victoria in recognition that the regiment escorted Prince Albert to the royal wedding in 1840.

The 17th Lancers were raised by Colonel John Hale, who devised the unique 'death's head' badge emblem and the motto 'Or Glory,' hence the famous nickname 'The Death or Glory Boys'.

Men in the small Russian fort protecting the harbour at Balaclava opened fire on the British invasion force as it approached but when Royal Navy ships fired a few salvos in return a white flag of surrender was raised almost at once.

A contemporary picture of the Charge of the Heavy Brigade at Balaclava, as the 2nd Dragoons on their distinctive grey horses smash their way through the ranks of the Russian cavalry. For their gallantry two NCOs of the regiment were awarded the Victoria Cross.

Panoramic view of the Light Brigade action looking across the north valley from the Fedioukine Heights.

The 11th Hussars plunged through the left flank of the Don Cossack field battery. The panic-stricken gunners tried to defend their field pieces by fending off the attackers with their rammers, but British sabres cut many of them down, hacking mercilessly at those who tried to get away. Others scurried under their guns to try to escape the attackers, only to be hunted out and cut to pieces.

Private Samuel Parkes was awarded the Victoria Cross for gallantry in trying to save a comrade. He was captured and was detained as a prisoner of war for a year. Light Dragoons wore a black beaver chaco and a dark blue double-breasted tunic decorated with gilt and gold cord. The dark blue overalls (trousers) had two gold lace stripes down the outer seam which indicated that they were light cavalry. All light cavalry units wore the less bulky ankle boots. (Adrian Bay)

A model image of Captain William Morris wearing the blue jacket and gold-peaked forage cap of a staff officer. A Devonian by birth, he had just recovered from a bout of cholera, and chose to accept command of the 17th Lancers when the opportunity arose to go into action. Known in the Light Brigade as 'The Pocket Hercules' he had gained the nickname 'Old Slats' while serving with the 16th Lancers in India, where he was wounded in action at the Battle of Aliwal. (Adrian Bay)

Lieutenant Edward Phillips, 8th Hussars, had his horse shot from under him and had to fight on foot, firing his revolver to great effect in all directions. Born in 1830 in London, on his retirement from the regular army he became an officer in the Ayrshire Yeomanry. He settled with his wife and family near Reading, where he died in 1915, aged 85. He was one of the last two surviving officers who had taken part in the Light Brigade action at Balaclava. As fate would have it at the time of his death British Expeditionary Forces were once again suffering the hardships of military campaigning in Europe and Turkey. (Adrian Bay)

The momentum took the leading rank right through the line of enemy guns and into the Russian cavalry, which was standing to horse at the rear, having been stunned into inactivity. The next line then came in and engaged the artillerymen, while some units veered to the right in order to take them in the flank and rear. A desperate hand-to-hand struggle ensued.

Poignant detail from the Lady Butler picture showing the look of relief in the eyes of the central figure as he looks towards the comparative safety of the British lines, while behind him a Lancer cradles a wounded trumpeter in his arms. Another man tries to steady an excited Light Dragoon charger, while in the background horses are still being hit by enemy fire or are simply collapsing from exhaustion. Note the scavenger birds in the distant sky already circling the battlefield.

Commemorative statue dedicated to Florence Nightingale in Waterloo Place, London. Many men who took part in the Light Brigade action were taken on board ships without being attended to by a doctor and transported to Scutari, where medical attention was minimal, the hospital was disorganised and filthy, wounds became infected and men died unnecessarily. After Florence Nightingale and her nurses arrived, the mortality rate improved.

The Crimea Medal with *Alma, Balaclava, Inkerman* and *Sebastopol* clasps, the Long Service Good Conduct Medal and the Turkish Medal.

Lieutenant Alexander Dunn was awarded the Victoria Cross for gallantry during the Light Brigade action at Balaclava. He had acquired a sabre which was much heftier than the regulation weapon and used it to great effect when trying to rescue his comrades who were being attacked by enemy horsemen.

Private William Pearson, 17th Lancers, was badly wounded at Balaclava when a lance pierced his lung. He was transported to the hospital at Scutari, where he suffered in dreadful conditions and his chances of survival seemed slim until he was placed under the personal care of Florence Nightingale, who even fitted him out with clothes for the journey back to England. However, due to rough conditions on board ship his health deteriorated, to such an extent that he opened his eyes one day to see two men trying on his boots and clothes because they thought he was dead. He eventually came under the care of a doctor in Malta who 'patched me up and made me fit for service again'. (Gordon Toye)

A native of Shropshire, John Ashley Kilvert, seen here resplendent in the dress uniform of the 11th Hussars, settled in Wednesbury in the West Midlands, where he gave most of his life to public service, including being appointed mayor of the town.

Seventy survivors of the Light Brigade action were invited to an all-expenses-paid visit to the Fleet Street offices of newspaper proprietor T. Harrison Roberts to witness Queen Victoria's Diamond Jubilee Procession in 1897. The sovereign is said to have stopped her carriage and acknowledged them with a wave of her hand.

The impressive memorial at the grave of three generations of the Short family in the Beckett Street Cemetery, Leeds – all were cavalrymen and all named Frederick. Our Frederick was awarded the DCM for his gallantry as 'One of the Six Hundred'. He was born at Windsor and on his retirement from the army he became an innkeeper at Chapel-Allerton, Leeds. He died in 1886, aged 61, and was buried at Kilmersdon in Somerset. His son served as an NCO with the 4th Light Dragoons and his grandson was killed in action at Naauwpoort, South Africa, in 1901 while serving with the 1st Royal Dragoons during the Boer War.

John Smith Parkinson spent the last years of his life in Yardley. He died in 1917 and he was buried with military honours at Yardley Cemetery, Birmingham. Amongst the estimated 400 people who were present at his funeral were representatives of the 11th Hussars, the Birmingham Police Force and the Birmingham Military Veterans' Association.

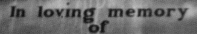

In loving memory
of
THOMAS EVERARD–HUTTON,
*Major 4th (Queen's Own) Light Drag*ns
died at Bath, June 10th 1896.
ONE OF THE "SIX HUNDRED."
Oct. 25th 1854.

"Thou hast covered my head in the day of battle."

Affectionately dedicated by his daughter.
M. T. E–H.

CANADA'S FIRST VICTORIA CROSS

Born in 1833 a short distance north of this site, Alexander Dunn was educated at Upper Canada College and at Harrow, England. In 1853 he was commissioned Lieutenant in the 11th Hussars. A participant in the charge of the Light Brigade at Balaclava on October 25, 1854, he saved the lives of two of his regiment by cutting down their Russian attackers, and thus became Canada's first winner of the newly-created Victoria Cross. In 1858 Dunn helped to raise the 100th Royal Canadian Regiment, which he later commanded. In 1864 he transferred to the 33rd (Duke of Wellington's) Regiment, and four years later was accidentally killed while hunting in Abyssinia.

Archaeological and Historic Sites Board of Ontario

Members of the Royal British Legion present their standards during the re-dedication service at the grave of Trumpeter William Smith, 11th Hussars, at St John's Parish Church, Knutsford. (John Lester)

Opposite top: The memorial plaque at Bath Abbey dedicated to Major Thomas Everard-Hutton by his daughters. Major Hutton retired by sale of commission in 1857. In 1864 he assumed the surname Everard-Hutton and resided at Middleton Hall, King's Lynn, and then at St Asaph, Denbighshire, North Wales. He spent the last years of his life living in a magnificent house at 7 The Circus, Bath. He died in 1896 and was buried with military honours at Locksbrook Cemetery, Bath. (Tim Day)

Opposite bottom: A commemorative plaque dedicated to Alexander Dunn VC was placed close to his family home in Toronto in 1966 and a plaque was placed in Clarence Square Park, at Spadina, Toronto. His medals are in the possession of Upper Canada College.

Colonel David Murray Brown and Major Patrick Timmons with Private Ferdinand Stanley's Crimea medals, which were presented to The Queen's Royal Hussars Museum in 2002. The medals were originally bequeathed to St Benedict's Church at Gorton in Manchester, on the death of Private Stanley in 1898, where they were encased in a panel in the wall of the church as a permanent memorial. However, when the church became derelict they were presented to the regimental museum. (The Queen's Royal Hussars)

Model of a life or death decision. Having bloodied their sabres, men of the 11th Hussars and 17th Lancers decide which direction to go to make their escape from marauding Cossacks, who were moving in to plunder the bodies of the dead, kill any Light Brigade stragglers and finish off the wounded. (Adrian Bay)

Palmer, who was unaware of the danger. Before Dunn could warn his fellow officer, Private Gregory Jowett swooped by and cut the Russian down, saving Palmer's life. When Lieutenant Dunn told Palmer what he had seen, Palmer recalled that a few days earlier he had caught Jowett asleep at his post and although this was a flogging offence, he had let him off with a caution. Perhaps this had been a fortunate decision as Jowett might not have been so inclined to risk his own life, had he been more severely punished.

Private Woodham had his horse shot from under him and it slumped to the ground trapping his left leg under its body. As he struggled to free himself a corporal of the 13th Light Dragoons rode up and started to tug at the animal's head in an effort to release him, causing the horse to twitch and move just enough for Private Woodham to drag himself free. He began running as fast as he could up the valley, with enemy riflemen taking pot shots at him as he did so. He came upon a trooper of the 8th Hussars lying trapped under his horse in much the same way as he had been and as he was hurrying past him the Hussar yelled desperately: 'For God's sake, man, don't

As men of the Light Brigade tried to help each other to get back to the British lines, many fell back from the main units and were taken prisoner by the Russians.

leave me here!' Private Woodham was understandably reluctant to put himself in any more danger after getting so near to salvation. He ran back nevertheless and tried to set the Hussar free, but the horse's lifeless body was too heavy. Sniper fire had now become relentless and as he squinted through the acrid smoke he could see enemy soldiers moving quickly towards him in the near distance; he had no choice but to leave the man to his fate. After joining a few other men and lying down pretending to be dead to try to fool the enemy marksmen, he eventually grabbed hold of the bridle of a loose Lancer horse, dragged himself up into the saddle with his last ounce of strength and drove the terrified beast up the valley.

Captain Morris, with about 20 men, had passed the Russian guns when they came upon a squadron of Russian Hussars. Ordering his men to keep together, he put his spurs into his mount 'Old Treasurer' and rode straight at the Russian leader, running him through with his sword up to the hilt with such force that he was unable to disengage his hand from his sword and they both fell to the ground. The Russians closed on him and slashed at him with their sabres, cutting through his forage cap, one blow penetrating his skull and he lost consciousness. Somehow he got to his feet and prepared to defend himself. A Cossack came up from his blind side and pierced his temple with the point of his lance. He became disorientated by the shock of the blow and he thought his end was near. An officer called for him to surrender. As he was in no position to defend himself, he gave up his sword.

He was taken prisoner, but the officer to whom he had surrendered disappeared and he was left at the mercy of the Cossacks who robbed him of everything they could get their hands on. However, in the confusion he managed to slip away and grab the reins of a riderless horse that dragged him off. Pursued by the Russians through the thick smoke of the battlefield, he caught another horse, which was shot and fell on him, trapping his leg, as had happened almost inevitably to so many other riders. When he came to, in agony from a broken right arm, broken ribs and three deep head wounds, he managed to free his leg and stagger towards the British lines. Now almost completely exhausted from effort and loss of blood he came across the body of Captain Nolan and lay down beside it. An attempt was made by Turkish troops to recover them both, but as Russian fire rained down on the Turks they dropped their burdens and bolted.

When a message was received by the 17th Lancers that their senior officer was lying on the battlefield in a dangerously exposed position and in a very serious condition, Sergeant Charles Wooden – who had ridden in the charge and had had his horse shot from under him – and Surgeon James Mouat of the 6th Dragoons, volunteered to leave the British lines to attend to him. They struck out under murderous enemy fire and at the mercy of Cossack lancers who were marauding all around, plundering the dead and finishing off the wounded. They managed to bind the officer's wounds and succeeded in stopping a severe haemorrhage, which would almost certainly have taken his life. They then managed to carry the captain to safety, and he survived the ordeal. Similar exploits by many more Lancers as they returned up the valley are worth recording.

Cornet George Wombwell, 17th Lancers, had his horse shot from under him and found himself among the carnage on foot. He mounted a stray horse and joined the second line of the Light Brigade as it came hurtling by. He reached the guns, where his horse became so exhausted that it refused to move no matter how he tried to encourage it with his spurs. Masked by the smoke and the confusion of the battle he managed to sneak past two squadrons of Cossack Lancers and he was feeling quite pleased with himself when he heard a fierce shout and five Cossacks came riding towards him with drawn sabres, ordering him to throw down his weapon. Seeing that resistance was useless he did as he was asked, after which his pistol was seized and he was dragged roughly from his horse. A Russian officer came up and asked him if he spoke French, which he did, and the officer told him not to be alarmed as they were only rough in their manners. Considering Wombwell to be a good prize as he was an officer, he was marched off towards the Russian lines between two of them, with the other three behind. Suddenly they found themselves close to the 11th Hussars and 4th Light Dragoons, still in a reasonably formed body; and when Captain Morris's horse suddenly appeared he saw his chance and quickly mounted the animal, bending his body well over the neck to protect him from any bullets as he rode away. The Cossacks did not dare to pursue him as they would have had to face the British horsemen, the rear of which Cornet Wombwell joined. He was with this unit when it forced its way through the Russian Lancers, and exchanged a few words with 'Peck' Webb as he was being carried from the battlefield, before he himself arrived at a place of safety.

Corporal Thomas Morley of the 17th Lancers was a rough-and-ready man, who had lost his lancer cap and his long hair was blowing in the breeze, making him somewhat conspicuous as he yelled at the top of his voice for the men within his view to rally on him. 'Coom 'ere! Coom 'ere! He bellowed. 'Fall in, lads! Fall in!' Among about 20 lancers who responded to him were TSM Abraham Ranson, Corporal Penn, and Privates Wightman and Marsh. With wild curses and oaths he encouraged his men and led them in an all-out attack against some Russian Hussars who were blocking their return.

During this confrontation Sergeant James Scarfe, 17th Lancers, had his horse killed from under him, and he scored his hands as he scraped along in the dirt. He tried to obtain a loose horse but his hands were ripped up 'like a piece of pork' and useless, he couldn't grab hold of the horse to stop it. He was attacked several times by Cossacks during which time he received sword cuts to his head, neck, thigh and hands, and he was slashed across the eyes with a sabre. When the 11th Hussars came by he was helped onto a spare horse and returned up the valley.

Private William Purvis, 17th Lancers, had his horse wounded, which fell on him, breaking three of his ribs. He lay unconscious until Private Thomas Chadwick of the 4th Dragoon Guards came to his assistance and offered his hand to pull him up into the saddle behind him, but Purvis was badly hurt and in too much pain to remount, so he clung for dear life to Chadwick's stirrup to get out of the valley.

As Corporal Penn made his way back up the valley he came upon Private Philip Murphy of his regiment, who was lying helpless on the ground with blood pouring from wounds to his head and face; he looked as if he also had some internal injuries. The Corporal managed to get him to his feet and offered his comrade a place behind him his saddle, but Murphy decided he would prefer to walk, which they did together; with Murphy making 'some quaint remarks' on the way.

Private William Pearson, 17th Lancers, managed to break through the line of enemy Lancers, but three Cossacks moved in to try to cut him off. He gave rein to his charger and with the momentum he succeeded in beating them off too. However, a

As the remnants of the 17th Lancers made their way back up the valley under heavy enemy fire, Sergeant Farrell stopped to hold Captain Webb's charger steady, as Sergeant Berryman helped their mortally wounded officer to the ground.

fourth Cossack wheeled across his path and prepared to attack him. He had taught his horse to respond to certain gestures, and as he pressed his knees together the charger reared up, threatening the Cossack with its front legs, forcing him to swerve away to miss the hooves as they came down. He eventually broke free and spurred his horse on. One of his assailants had jabbed him in the side with his lance and although it did not trouble him at first, the point had penetrated his lung and he eventually collapsed from severe pain and loss of blood.

Private William Gardiner, 13th Light Dragoons, had been disabled when a round shot fractured his leg, and he had fallen behind in danger of being caught by advancing Russian cavalry. Sergeant Henry Ramage had moved forward with the Scots Greys and he saw Private Gardiner in difficulties. He dashed out from the ranks, and dismounting, he lifted the stricken soldier from his horse. Under very heavy enemy fire from several directions, he carried him to the rear of the Cavalry lines, thereby saving his life, as the area where the incident occurred was soon afterwards overrun by a squadron of enemy cavalry.

Captain Soame Jenyns had seen his friend, Captain Thomas Howard Goad, gallop to within 100 yards of the guns but the smoke became too thick and he lost sight of him. Later Captain Goad was seen on foot. Private Stephen Farrington spotted him sitting down with his revolver in his hand, having been wounded in the lower part of his face. He was last seen surrounded by Cossack lancers. Captain Jenyns therefore became the senior surviving officer of the 13th Light Dragoons. He led a small unit of his men back up the valley and out of action. His horse, Moses, was struggling with a bullet wound in the shoulder and another bullet that had entered via the hip and embedded itself in the guts.

Several other men of the 13th Light Dragoons had similar experiences as they dragged their way back up the valley. RSM George Gardner got to the mouth of the Russian guns when a cannon ball smashed into his horse's chest and the impact threw him into the air. When he recovered he found himself sprawled across a Russian gun. He scrambled down and ran all the way back up the valley.

Private Mitchell, sword in hand, found himself in the midst of a shower of bullets. Private Charles Pollard came up and threw himself down behind the carcass of a horse to shelter from the bullets and called to Mitchell to join him. Mitchell suggested they had better make their way back immediately. They had not gone far when a man of their regiment who was trapped beneath his dead charger called to them for help. He was covered in blood streaming from a severe wound to his head; they managed to draw his leg from under the horse but his thigh was broken. On seeing his injuries they laid him down. Realising he was beyond hope, the trooper said: 'Look out for yourselves!'

Mitchell eventually became separated from Private Pollard. As he carried on, Lord Cardigan came galloping up from the direction of the guns, and on meeting the stranded trooper he pulled up and after enquiring about his horse he said that he had better get back as fast as he could or he would be taken prisoner. As he reached a piece of ground that was very loose and made the going even harder, he was dismayed to see the Scots Greys about 500 yards from him in the act of retiring at a trot. He could see a party of Cossacks to his right intending to cut off some of the dismounted men, but a party of Chasseurs D'Afrique showed themselves menacingly and the Cossacks rode away. He then fell in with a trooper of the Scots Greys who was standing but had been blinded by a shell wound. He bound his head with a handkerchief and began to lead him to safety. Arriving near number 4 redoubt they asked for some water and an officer of the 68th Light Infantry gave them some rum. Soon afterwards they reached the British lines and the man of the Scots Greys was taken to the ambulances.

As Cornet Hugh Montgomery was making his way back up the valley he tried to keep himself from the view of enemy horsemen that he could hear shouting all around him by hiding in the clouds of smoke that hung in pockets everywhere. However, he was seen by a party of six enemy Hussars. Turning to face them he presented his pistol and as they came on into the attack he shot four in quick succession. He then drew his sabre from its scabbard, and using it like a man possessed he raced forward at the other two and slashed wildly at them, forcing them to turn their horses and bolt. Feeling justly pleased with his fighting prowess, he met up with a few more stragglers and was walking back with them when he saw two of his men being attacked by a superior number of Russians. He went to assist them, but as he did so a party of enemy horsemen loomed out of the smoke. Before he realised the danger, one of them raised his pistol and shot the British officer in the neck. Cornet Montgomery fell to the ground, never to rise again.

Lieutenant Percy Smith, although unarmed, was giving 'an example of steadiness'. He found himself separated from his men and was suddenly surrounded by three Cossacks. One of them made a lance thrust at him, which he pushed aside with his bridle arm, receiving a scratch from the edge of the blade. A second Cossack made a lance thrust he could not parry effectively without dropping his reins. The point of the lance pierced his ribs, but the officer jumped on his assailant before he could perform the coup de grace and lance and man tumbled to the ground. A party of 11th Hussars came to the rescue and dispersed the rest of the enemy. As he was making his way back on foot Smith passed Cornet Denzil Chamberlayne sitting on his dead horse, Pimento. Chamberlayne asked Smith what he should do and the officer told him that it would be best to remove the saddle and bridle and try to get back, for it would be easier to get another mount than to acquire new horse furniture. Chamberlayne placed the saddle on his head and started off up the valley. His powers of endurance and sang froid were tested to the full as he threaded his way precariously through parties of marauding Cossacks who eyed him suspiciously. He managed to hold his nerve and the enemy soldiers let him pass because they thought he was a fellow pillager.

Having cut and thrust his way through the Russian lancers, Private Robert Nichol,

'All That Was Left of Them'. Lady Elizabeth Butler (1844–1933) painted many popular military pictures. This famous painting of the survivors of the Light Brigade returning from the momentous action was produced the year after the first Balaclava reunion banquet. It is unlikely that the events depicted all happened at the same time, but the artist took great care over details and several survivors who posed for her appear in the picture. The original painting is housed at the Manchester City Art Gallery.

8th Hussars, stopped to assist Private John Keen of the 13th Light Dragoons, who was wounded and horseless. Private Nichol dismounted and helped the stricken trooper onto his own horse, and he and Private Stephen Harrison, 13th Light Dragoons, conveyed him back to the British lines.

Almost back at the lines, Private Doyle came in contact with Colonel Shewell, who was in danger of becoming bogged down in the ploughed ground. Doyle knew the ground well, and being on a pathway, he shouted for the officer to get back on the track, or he would never get across. Shewell took his advice. When Doyle got back no one recognised him as he was covered with blood. His comrades knew the horse and the same Colonel Shewell whom he had just directed called out for him to identify himself. This done, Shewell told him to take his horse to the commissary officer. He instructed him to shoot the horse, as he thought the beast was done for. Private Doyle had no intention of having Hickabod put down and later stated: 'I would have soon have lost my own life as to have shot my horse, who had so gallantly carried me through the vicissitudes of that eventful but glorious day. The wound healed rapidly, and by the Battle of Inkerman my horse was as well as ever.' On inspection he discovered that he had five buttons blown off his dress jacket, the slings of his sabretache were cut off, and the right heel and spur of his boot was blown off. No less than 27 bullets had lodged in his rolled cloak. As for the lance prod he had received to his forehead, he 'did not know there was a hole in it for a week afterwards.'

Private Bird's horse was hit during the advance and it stumbled to the ground, but by a 'skilful movement' he landed on his feet unhurt. He caught a horse belonging to the Scots Greys and rejoined his troop. As the remnants of the brigade charged the enemy Lancers who had blocked their retreat he received a bullet wound through the calf of his right leg and a lance wound in his arm. His horse was shot and fell on him trapping his left leg. He was at once surrounded by the enemy and thought that he would be killed. There was an officer present who controlled the situation and with several other Light Brigade men he was marched down the valley and into captivity.

Private Badger had been attacked by two gunners, one of whom stabbed him in the side. On his return up the valley he came upon Captain Oldham, who had been thrown from his horse after it had been struck by a shell. Although he was unhurt, he was bowled over almost immediately by a musket-ball. He called Badger across and asked him to take his personal belongings but as Badger moved towards him another ball struck the officer and he fell back dead, still clutching the watch and purse he was holding out. On seeing some Cossacks advancing, Badger caught the stirrup of

Florence Nightingale – 'The Lady with the Lamp' – and 36 nurses arrived at Scutari Hospital on the day the Battle of Inkerman was fought. They overcame petty jealousies among the military doctors and the lack of facilities to reorganise the hospital wards and eventually bring some measure of cleanliness and comfort to the patients.

William Howard Russell was sent to the Crimea to report on the campaign for *The Times* newspaper. His unbiased views of the Light Brigade action and conditions in the camps and hospitals are masterpieces of journalism and brought the true horrors of war to the attention of the British public.

a straggler of the 13th but due to his wound he was unable to run fast enough and had to let go. However, the Cossacks stopped by the dead officer to loot the body and he was able to make his escape. He made it back at the British lines, stumbling in with his uniform soaked in blood from the wound in his side. Captain Winters' wounded horse was the first back to the British lines, and Private Badger was the last of the 13th Light Dragoons to arrive back.

TSM Loy Smith had just congratulated himself for having got beyond the lancers when his charger began to limp. Sergeant John Joseph warned him that his horse's leg was broken and he just managed to eject himself from the saddle before the animal slumped to the ground. He immediately started running for his life back up the valley. Several of his men galloped for their lives past him, some encouraged him to keep going, but the enemy were all around them and none of them had time to stop to assist him. Not wishing to get trampled in the stampede he moved to the left side of the valley close to the Causeway and eventually all the mounted men had disappeared into the distance.

He slogged on with his sword in his hand, with bullets whizzing through the air above him or puncturing the ground all around him; he thought that one of them was sure to hit their target eventually. He could hardly breathe with the exertion by the time two Cossacks came galloping up behind him. He gave up all hope of escaping and decided that they were not going to kill him without a fight. However, they veered to their right and made two mounted troopers of the 11th Hussars their target instead.

Lord Paget later wrote: 'And what a scene of havoc was this last mile – strewn with the dead and dying, and all friends! Some running, some limping, some crawling; horses in every position of agony, struggling to get up, then floundering again on their mutilated riders!'

Several men of the 4th Light Dragoons claimed to be the last to get back to the British lines to answer to the roll call. Sergeant Howes made this claim, as did John Edden, who in later life lived only a few miles away from Howes. Private John Palin claimed to be the last 'mounted' man to return of the Light Brigade, where he discovered that his rolled cloak was riddled with bullet holes and two balls had passed through his water flask. TSM Loy Smith, 'burning with indignation at what had happened', remembered riding in on a horse belonging to the 4th Light Dragoons, and after handing it back to its rightful regiment, he joined the remnants of his own unit and numbered off as 63. 'Thus it is evident that the 11th was the last regiment, and I the last man, that returned up the valley.'

Lord Cardigan addressed fewer than 200 men that managed to answer the roll call, with the promise: 'Men you have done a glorious deed. England will be proud of you, and grateful to you. If you live to get home, be sure you will be provided for. Not one of you fellows will have to seek refuge in a workhouse.'

The number of horses lying about with their entrails scattered around them was fearful. There were several chargers with empty saddles galloping aimlessly about the valley. The earth was sodden with blood where groups of mangled bodies lay, with severed heads, arms and legs lying all over the ground. The final Light Brigade casualty list was believed to be 113 killed and 134 wounded, with the loss of 475 horses.

Stragglers came in at various times throughout the day. Private William Butler of the 17th Lancers had been out all night exposed to the elements before being discovered by a French sentry next day. As he had been making his way back he was attacked by two Cossacks. He managed to defend himself and kill them both, but in doing so he received severe cuts to his face and hand. His horse was shot dead and he eventually lost consciousness from loss of blood.

In spite of their fearful losses the Light Brigade was still kept on alert until about 5 o'clock that day before being allowed to go back to their camp. As darkness fell that night the survivors tried to settle their nerves and get some rest in half-empty tents: 'The camp seemed quite deserted, and the shadow of death lay heavy upon it.' Some tents had not a single man in them. Did those men dare to take satisfaction from the gallant thing they knew they had done? What would the British public think of them? Indeed, would they ever get to know? Some wrestled with remorse remembering how in the heat of the battle they had been given no choice but to leave comrades to their fate. If they managed to drift into a restless sleep, they did so 'thinking of our dead and absent friends.'

At the back of some minds was the thought that they would have to make the melancholy journey to the devastated parents of their friends to inform them that their sons were dead. Ted Woodham was already contemplating the trip to Herefordshire to give the bad news to the widow of George Wootton.

Official figures for the numbers of men who were killed or died of wounds during and after the Light Brigade action vary. I have compiled the following based on information included in the relevant publications recorded in the bibliography. The fallen were:

4th Light Dragoons

Killed in Action
Major John Thomas Douglas Halkett, Lieutenant Henry Astley (Arthur) Sparke, Troop Sergeant-Major Frank Herbert, Sergeants Edward Campbell and Richard Lynch, Corporal Henry Spence (Spencer), Trumpeters Edward Barnes and Thomas Lovelock, Privates James Donaldson, Daniel Haxhall, Thomas Hulton, Charles Marshall, Henry Moody, Michael Phelan, George Robinson, George Swan, Thomas Tomsett and Charles Waight.

Died of Wounds
Privates Joseph Phillips, William R. Sutcliffe and Joseph Whitby.

Died in Captivity
Troop Sergeant-Major William Fowler, Sergeant William Thomas, Privates Thomas Fletcher, George Linser and James Narmoyle.

8th Hussars

Killed in Action

Captain George Lockwood, Lieutenant, Viscount John Charles Henry Fitzgibbon, Cornet George Clowes, Troop Sergeant-Major Henry 'Harry' McCluer, Sergeants Michael Reilly and William Williams, Corporal William Donald, Privates Joshua Adams, John Barry, Michael Brennan, James Dies, Francis Finnegan, John Fitzgibbon, Dennis Hanrahan, Thomas Hefferon, Edmund Herbert, Martin Lennon, Edward McDonald, George Morris, Edward Turner, Charles Waterer and John White.

Died of Wounds
Sergeant Edward T. Sewell, Corporal John Sewell, Trumpeter John William Dunn, Privates Francis Bray, John Brown, Joseph Ross and William Ryan.

11th Hussars

Killed in Action
Sergeants John Jones and Thomas Jordan, Corporal Thomas France, Privates Charles Allured, Joseph Brunton, Robert Bubb, Charles B. Cooper, William Davies, James Elder, Reuben Gwinnell, George Hoarne, John Jackman, James Larkin, Robert Layzell, Robert levett, John McGeorge, David Purcell, Archibald Russell, Leonard Shoppee, Thomas Shrive, James Stephenson, Henry J. Wakelin, David Ward, William Wareham and George Wootton.

Died of Wounds
Lieutenant George Powell Houghton, Corporal Edward Hudson, Privates Wilson Firth, John C. Purvis, John Strutt, William Taylor and George Turner.

Died in Captivity
Corporal James Williams, Privates John Berry and Walter Hyde.

13th Light Dragoons

Killed in Action

Captains John Augustus Oldham and Thomas Edward Goad, Cornet Hugh Montgomery, Troop Sergeant-Major John Weston, Corporal Edward W. Aubrey Smith, Privates Thomas Blackett, Charles Court, William Dorrell, Robert Fraser, Algernon Holliday, William Lawson, James Slattery, James Watson and Thomas Joseph Williams.

Died of Wounds
Private Henry Pegler

Died in Captivity
Trumpeter William Howarth, Privates William Henry Bainton and William Martin.

17th Lancers

Killed in Action
Captain John Pratt Winter, Lieutenant John Henry Thompson, Sergeant Edward Talbot, Privates William Baker, William Barker, Walter Brooks, George Broom, Thomas Corcoran, Richard Dollard, Patrick Dowling, George Flowers, Henry Grey, Robert Jackson, John Lees, Robert Ling, Edward Loftus, Robert McNeill, Frederick Melrose, John Mitton, Henry Pearce, Johnson Sewell, James Stannage, John Wilson and Constantine Wrigley.

Died of Wounds
Captain Augustus Frederick Cavendish Webb, Corporal George Taylor, Trumpeter William Brittain, Privates Frederick Clifford and John Gravernor.

Died in Captivity
Corporal James Hall, Privates Thomas Brown, Robert Edge, Henry Ellis, William Harrison, Alfred Jenner, William Kirk, George Liles, Thomas Sharpe and Henry M. Young.

5

AND THE REST IS HISTORY

'The fewer men, the greater share of honour.'

HENRY V

During the next few days several men were sent to the Russian lines under a flag of truce. Trumpeter Joy, limping from an injury to his leg, went with 'necessaries' for captured officers and to request time to bury the British dead. He was brought before General Pavel Liprandi, who ordered that refreshments be put before him. Private Samuel Jamieson, 11th Hussars, whose real name was Murdock, was not quite so well received. He was approaching the enemy lines under a flag of truce when several shots were fired at him. Some bullets went through the flag, the ears of his horse were ripped off by slugs, and a bullet smashed into his leg, where it remained for a long time. (On a different occasion, he was helping a wounded Russian to a drink when the Russian treacherously thrust at him with his bayonet and wounded him on the forehead.)

About 60 men were held by the Russians as prisoners of war. Private Farquharson was marched to the end of the valley and there he was searched by 'a particularly ill-favoured looking dog', who ransacked his haversack and tied him up so tight that he almost fainted with the pain. He was treated very brutally, being constantly beaten, thrashed and prodded with lances. He was tied to a rein at the back of a horse and dragged across country as fast as his legs could carry him; which included being pulled across a river and nearly drowned. On one occasion he was forced to stand

Several Light Brigade men were present at Horse Guards Parade in London on 18 May 1856, when Queen Victoria presented campaign medals to veterans of the Crimean War. In the bath chair is Sir Thomas Troubridge, who lost a leg and a foot at Inkerman. The picture was produced by Sir John Tenniel, who later became famous for his illustrations of Lewis Carroll's 'Alice' books.

beneath a tree where a noose had been prepared and was threatened with hanging, while Cossacks mocked him. He was only saved when a Russian officer took charge of the situation. On another occasion, having become drunk on beer and vodka, he wanted to fight with some Cossacks who were trying to search him but fortunately someone picked him up and carried him away from his angry tormentors. Next day he woke up in a barn full of English prisoners. It had been Private Parkes who had carried him away from the danger. During the journey to Simferopol they came across a man they suspected was a deserter and a spy, so Private Parkes took it upon himself to knock him senseless with a punch on the nose.

At Simferopol the wounds of many men were mortifying, and most had lost so much blood that their clothes stiffened and could be stood on end. Private John Dryden, 11th Hussars, had 36 wounds all over his body, while Privates William Cooper and Robert Duke of the 13th Light Dragoons had nearly as many. Privates

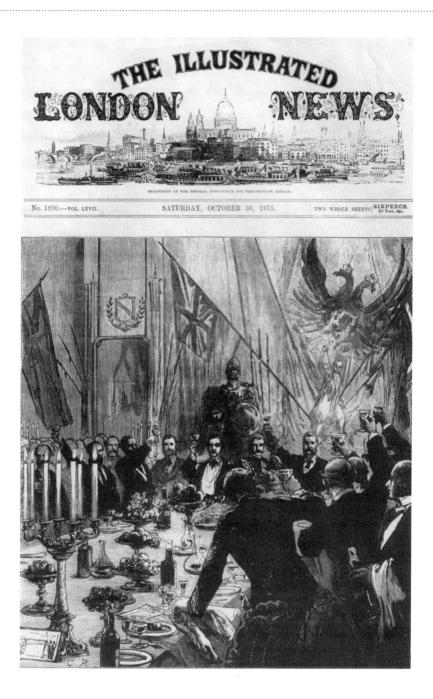

The front cover of the *Illustrated London News,* which reported on the first Balaclava banquet held at the Alexandra Palace in 1875. Veterans who had taken part in the Light Brigade action were interviewed for the newspaper and it was found that some had become in-pensioners at the Chelsea Hospital, while many more had fallen on hard times. It was decided to form a Balaclava Commemoration Society, which came into being in1877. In 1879 the society restricted its members to those who had taken part in the Light Brigade action at Balaclava.

Thomas Fletcher and James Normoyle, 4th Light Dragoons, were terribly mutilated, the latter having a sword cut across his face which had nearly split it in two. They both died of their injuries.

Private Wightman spoke of how four men died after having their limbs amputated with nothing more to ease the agony than having water poured over their heads. Out of nine men who had limbs removed at Simferopol only one survived the dreadful ordeal. 'It seemed a butchery job, and certainly was a sickening sight.' William Baynton, 13th Light Dragoons, received nine wounds, which included a serious injury to his leg. He was one of the men who died at Simferopol. His brother, Harry Powell, received a letter from him stating how kind the Russians were and how well he had been looked after by the Sisters of Mercy. Private Thomas Cook, 13th Light Dragoons, had received a severe gunshot wound. The bullet drove a button from his tunic into his chest, which perhaps saved his life.

As the day wore on the suffering from their wounds increased. 'At that time, owing to excitement and one thing and another, you don't feel the wounds that you receive; but when your blood has cooled down a bit, and you are in a calmer frame of mind, you begin to feel the wounds.' Private John Bevin, 8th Hussars, was having his wounds dressed when he noticed a Russian cavalryman staring at him from the other side of the hut. The man had two dreadful sword cuts on his head and three fingers missing. He came over to Bevin and accused him of causing his terrible wounds. Bevin confirmed that this was the case in an unconcerned manner; pointing to a fragment of his own right ear, he gave the Russian to understand that it was he who had caused his injury, and managed to talk his way out of the difficult situation.

Later that day General Liprandi paid them a visit, and asked what alcohol they had drunk which had made them '...come down and attack them in such a mad manner?' Private William Kirk, 17th Lancers, was leaning against the door having had a few vodkas since arriving at the hut, and replied that had they been drinking that morning: '...we would have taken half Russia by this time.' Liprandi was amused and agreed. 'Private Parkes told Lord Paget: 'My Lord, the officers were not ashamed of being seen walking about with us.'

TSM William Fowler, 4th Light Dragoons, was sitting in the corner, having been run through the back with a lance. 'A dignified soldier' and 'one of the handsomest men in the Light Brigade', he struggled to his feet and after reprimanding Kirk for his impertinence towards an officer, he assured Liprandi that none of them had seen food or drink that day. The General was impressed, and after complimenting them as 'gallant fellows', he promised to provide them with pens and paper so they could write to their families back home.

The relatively fit men were allowed to attend to the wounded as best they could that day and on the following one the seriously injured were separated and transported to the hospital at Simferopol. To give more room to his comrades with leg injuries in the rough carts that were taking them, TSM Fowler walked every step of the 50 miles,

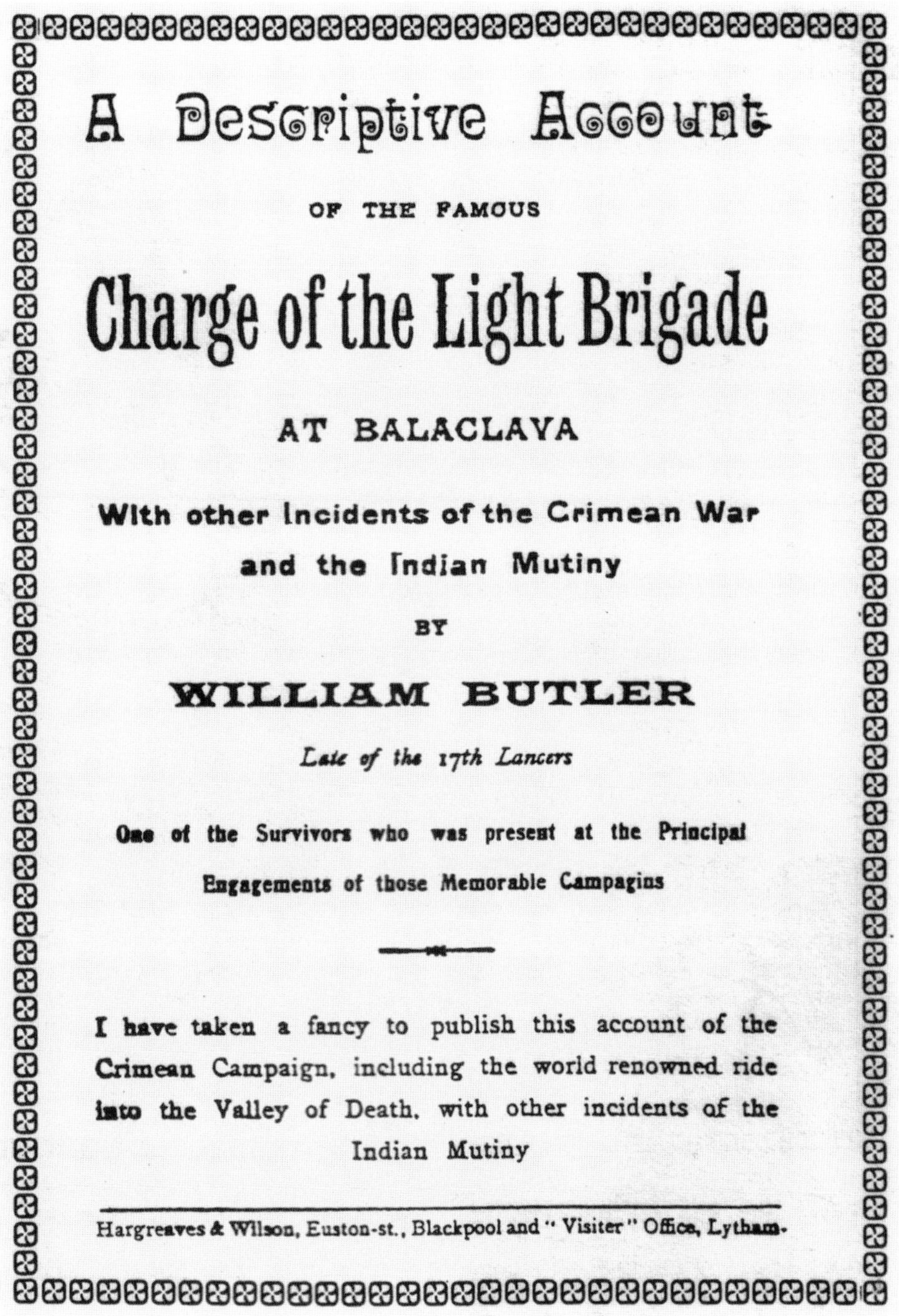

A Descriptive Account

OF THE FAMOUS

Charge of the Light Brigade

AT BALACLAVA

With other Incidents of the Crimean War and the Indian Mutiny

BY

WILLIAM BUTLER

Late of the 17th Lancers

One of the Survivors who was present at the Principal
Engagements of those Memorable Campagins

———

I have taken a fancy to publish this account of the
Crimean Campaign, including the world renowned ride
into the Valley of Death, with other incidents of the
Indian Mutiny

Hargreaves & Wilson, Euston-st., Blackpool and " Visiter" Office, Lytham.

The title page of the account produced by Lancashire veteran trooper William Butler of the 17th Lancers.

A group of survivors of the Light Brigade pose for a picture during one of the many reunions they enjoyed. Major John Berryman VC is on the back row, far left, balancing rather awkwardly on a chair.

Survivors of the Light Brigade pose for a group photograph at the annual dinner held at St James's Restaurant, London, on 25 October 1906.

Three Nottingham veteran Chargers pictured seated at the front in this marvellous photograph: Matthew Holland on the left, George Watson in the middle, and Thomas Morley on the right. The photograph was taken at Skegness in 1905. (John Beckworth).

which severely aggravated his wound and he died soon afterwards. At Simferopol Private Kirk was placed, stupidly, perhaps maliciously, in the same ward as many Russian soldiers who had been wounded and maimed at the Battle of Inkerman. Kirk was spat on by two of them, and he bravely went at them with his fists. He was eventually overpowered by the orderlies, who placed him in a restraining jacket and tied him to his bed. He was released that night with the warning that he would be severely dealt with if he resorted to violence again. He died soon afterwards; it was suspected that he had been poisoned.

In many cases during long journeys the prisoners were billeted in filthy huts and Privates Wightman and Thomas Brown, 17th Lancers, caught raging fevers. They were left in the hospital at Alexandrovska, where Private Brown died two days after being admitted. He was the cousin of Private William Pearson, who rode in the charge with the 4th Light Dragoons.

Their final destination was to be Odessa. On the march to the town they arrived at a village where there was nothing to eat. Privates Bird and Cooper and a man named Chapman of the 4th Dragoon Guards were sent to a village across the river to get some provisions. As they were waiting for the boat to bring them back, they were attacked by three men with clubs, who beat them to the floor. As 'there were not three finer

'Death or Glory' ex-cavalryman, William Pearson, in a casual pose resplendent in his campaign medals from the Crimea and India with members of the cycling club outside the local bicycle makers and repair shop at Davygate, York. (Gordon Toye)

men in the British Cavalry' they retaliated aggressively, and the antagonists eventually fled the scene. However, next day the three recognised the men who assaulted them among the soldiers of the port, their battered and bruised faces gave them away. The British were preparing to take their revenge when the Russians fixed bayonets to warn them off. They demanded the officer arrest the six men, but he refused, so Private Bird knocked him to the ground. Some of the British grabbed the bayonets with their bare hands while others ran to a hut and armed themselves with stakes pulled from the roof. The Russian officer ordered his men to load with ball-cartridges, fully intent on firing them, and as the British had no firearms they backed off. It was later reported to the Governor, and the men are said to have been punished.

Their stay in Odessa was mainly a happy one. Some prisoners set up a theatre company to pass the time, with Trumpeter Crawford and Boatswain Jack West leading the band. Private Tom Lucas: 'who was naturally of somewhat effeminate appearance' playing the female parts, and Private Charlie Warren of the 13th Light Dragoons acted as a clown. Local dignitaries and townsfolk waved them off as they left captivity on British troopships under a flag of truce on 23 October. They disembarked at Kadikoi on 26 October, just over a year after the action at Balaclava. Men who returned were shown on a nominal roll made out at the Cavalry Depot, Scutari, on 9 November 1855, as being prisoners of war, there from 4 November. The formality of being tried for being absent without leave by a garrison court-martial at Scutari took place on 10 November 1855. They were 'charged' with 'having been taken a prisoner of war at Balaclava' during the Charge of the Light Brigade – they were 'honourably acquitted.'

On 5 November 1854, the 'Soldiers' Battle' was fought among mist and fog at Inkerman. After seven hours of fierce fighting, over 10,000 men had been killed or wounded. On the same day as the Battle of Inkerman, Florence Nightingale and her

Seven veteran cavalrymen of the 17th Lancers. The picture accompanied the sketches of the men which appeared in the *Illustrated London News* at the time of the first Balaclava banquet. Standing at the back is Charles Aldous, who was wounded, and seated from the left are Joseph Ireland, who died in Manchester in 1899; William G. Cattermole, who was wounded, and died in 1884; Henry Joy, who received the DCM for his part in the action and died in 1893; George Weatherley, who died in 1885; James Scarfe, who was wounded, and died in 1886; and Thomas Dyer, who died less than a year after this picture was taken. There is some doubt that Ireland took part in the action because this is the only reunion he ever attended; he was the last survivor of this little group of heroes.

The grave of Joseph Malone, who died suddenly in the Officers' Mess of the 6th Dragoons in Pinetown, South Africa. The inscription on the memorial stone reads: 'In memory of Captain J. Malone, VC Riding Master, 6th Inniskilling Dragoons, who died at Pinetown, June 28th 1883, aged 50 years. He served throughout the Eastern campaign of 1854–55 and was one of the Six Hundred at Balaclava, October 25th 1854.' (Ian Knight)

FESTIVAL OF BRITAIN 1951
TRUMPET MAJOR
WILLIAM SMITH
1822-1879
WHO SOUNDED THE CHARGE AT
BALACLAVA LIVED HERE
THIS ROAD WAS FORMERLY KNOWN
AS LOVE LANE

During the Festival of Britain celebrations in 1951 a commemoration plaque was placed at the former home of Trumpeter William Smith in Knutsford, Cheshire, in what is now Stanley Road.

complement of dedicated nurses arrived to bring some comfort and cleanliness – though nowhere near enough of the latter to make a real difference – to the wounded. Undernourished British troops continued to suffer in the harsh Crimean winter. On the night of 14–15 November about 30 ships in the harbour at Balaclava were caught up in a storm and floundered, with the loss of all the winter clothing and medical supplies. Boots were packed 80 to a package, and some of these were all for the same foot! As winter set in, driving rain and piercing winds blew away tents and hospital marquees and turned the tracks into unusable quagmires. Freezing temperatures caused the deaths of many men and horses in miserable situations of exposure.

Private Butler:

We were ordered from the front in December 1854, for both men and horses were starving. The horses were actually eating each other, whilst the men were frostbitten. The food comprised green berries of coffee, and there was no fire to cook anything. I did not care if I lived or not. I have often had to be dug up with a spade, my hair being frozen to the tent. I shall never forget Christmas Day, 1854. I was nearly dead with hunger and filth, and I wished to die, but my time had not come.

The funeral cortege of Sergeant-Major Richard Hall Williams making its way to St Mark's Parish Church at Worsley near Manchester. He attended several reunions, his last one being in 1908. He died two years later, at the grand old age of 91. He was buried with military honours. There were many Freemasons at his funeral.

The programme for the service of thanksgiving held at Worsley Parish Church on 20 October 2004 to celebrate the life of local hero Richard Hall Williams and to commemorate the 150th anniversary of the Light Brigade action at Balaclava. The author attended the service, during which the church bell tolled 118 times to mark the number of men said to have been killed in the action. A recording of Trumpeter Lanfried sounding the charge was played. Sergeant Williams' great-grandson stated: 'He spent so much time public speaking, reciting the poem and going to dinners, that he didn't really spend a great deal of time with his family. He was definitely a local celebrity!' (Jim Glithero)

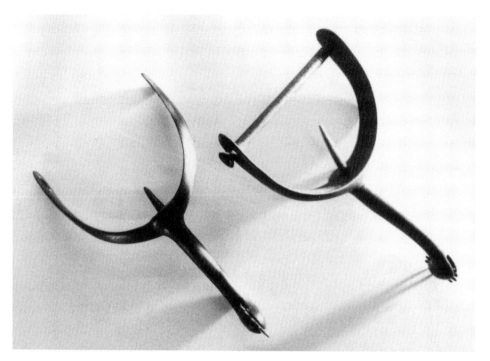

Spurs worn by Private David Andrews of the 11th Hussars during the Light Brigade action, still in the possession of his family. (The Andrews family)

After six bombardments and two assaults on a Sebastopol strong-point called the Redan, made on 18 June and 8 September 1855, which were costly in lives on both sides of the parapets, the Russians evacuated the city. The war was brought to an unsatisfactory end by the Treaty of Paris in February 1856. The first 111 Victoria Crosses were awarded for the campaign, and Roger Fenton's photographs, although not particularly graphic in terms of the horrors of the battlefield and the hospitals, were the first ever to be taken in a war zone. Newspaper reports, poems and books told the story and a public outcry followed their publication, part of the reason why Lord Aberdeen's Government was brought down.

On 3 March 1855, Queen Victoria visited several Light brigade survivors at Brompton Barracks in Chelsea, where she told her soldiers for the first time about a new award for bravery she was having commissioned, and the first recipients would be men who had fought and suffered in the Crimean War. The Victoria Cross is Britain's highest award for valour and is considered by many to be the most prestigious in the world. It takes precedence over all other orders, decorations and medals. It may be awarded to a person of any rank in any service and to civilians under military command, and to members of the armed forces of various Commonwealth countries and previous British Empire territories.

The VC was instituted by a Royal Warrant of Queen Victoria towards the end of the Crimean War on 29 January 1856, which stipulated 'that the cross shall only be awarded for conspicuous bravery, or some daring or pre-eminent act of valour or self-sacrifice or extreme devotion to duty in the presence of the enemy.' and men who fought in the Crimean campaign became the first recipients. The sovereign took a great interest in the award and in the design of the medal, suggesting that the original motto: *For the Brave* would lead to the inference that only those who have won the cross are considered brave and suggested that *For Valour* would be more suitable – she was right of course!

The names of the first recipients were announced in the *London Gazette* of 24 February 1857. Four men on the list had been awarded the medal for action at Balaclava. These four were present at the first investiture which took place in Hyde Park, London, on 26 June 1857, when Queen Victoria pinned 62 medals to the chests of the men who had gained it in the Crimean War; in at least one case she did actually pin the medal to the man's skin! The four Balaclava men were: 15th in line, Sergeant-Major John Grieve, 2nd Dragoons; 16th: Private Samuel Parkes, 4th Light Dragoons; 17th: Lieutenant Alexander Dunn, 11th Hussars; and 18th: 735 Troop Sergeant-Major John Berryman, 17th Lancers. Nine men were awarded the VC for valour at Balaclava, the other announcement dates being: 25 September 1857 to 1440 Corporal Joseph Malone, 13th Light Dragoons; 20 November 1857 to 795 Sergeant John Farrell, 17th Lancers; 2 June 1858 to Sergeant Henry Ramage, 2nd Dragoons, and Surgeon James Mouat, 6th Dragoons; 26 October 1858 to 799 Sergeant Charles Wooden, 17th Lancers.

The Commanding Officer of the 13th Light Dragoons was given a VC to be presented to the man considered to be the most deserving of the regiment to receive it, but as Corporal Malone and Private Lamb had been involved in the same incident he could not make up his mind which one of them to give it to. It was decided that they should draw lots for it. Corporal Malone was the elder of the two and got to draw first, and drew the lucky straw.

The award to Sergeant Wooden proved to be controversial. His name was not put forward at first, although Dr Mouat was. Wooden wrote to the doctor saying that if Mouat was to receive a VC then so should he, as he had been at the doctor's side during the rescue of Colonel Morris. Dr Mouat agreed and wrote to the Horse Guards supporting his claim. The reply to his letter reads:

His Royal Highness feels very unwilling to bring any further claim for the Victoria Cross for an act performed at so distant a period but as the decoration has been conferred on Dr James Mouat for the part he took in the rescue of Colonel Morris, and Sergeant Major Wooden appears to have acted in a manner very honourable to him on the occasion and, by his gallantry, been equally instrumental in saving the life of this officer, His Royal Highness is induced to submit the case.

Biographies of the nine men who were awarded the Victoria Cross
for valour at the Battle of Balaclava

JOHN GRIEVE was born on 3 May 1821 at Musselburgh near Edinburgh, East
Lothian, Scotland. A descendant of his wrote: 'As a young man he ran through a
small fortune.' He received his VC at the first investiture in 1857, and for his service
in the East he also received the Crimea Medal with *Balaclava, Inkerman* and *Sebastopol*
clasps, the Turkish Medal and the Medaille Militaire (France). Charles Dickens wrote
about his heroic deed in one of the first issues of his journal *All the Year Round*.
'He was offered a commission, and coming into more money he accepted.' He was
appointed Adjutant of the Scots Greys on 18 February 1859.

   John died on 1 December 1873, aged 52, at 26 New Bigging, Inveresk, Midlothian,
and he was buried in an unmarked family grave at St Michael's Churchyard at Old
Inveresk. A memorial stone was placed at the grave by representatives of the 2nd
Dragoons and the Royal Highland Fusiliers in 2003. His medals are at the Art Gallery
of South Australia in Adelaide.

   His great-nephew, Robert Cuthbert Grieve (1889–1957), was awarded the
Victoria Cross while serving during the Great War with the 37th Battalion (Victoria),
Australian Imperial Forces, at the Battle of Messines, Belgium, in 1917.

Henry Ramage VC.

HENRY RAMAGE was born in 1827 at Morningside,
Edinburgh, but there is very little known about his life.
His award of the Victoria Cross was Gazetted at the same
time as Surgeon Mouat. For his service in the East he
also received the Crimea Medal with *Balaclava, Inkerman*
and *Sebastopol* clasps, and the Turkish Medal. Henry
died not long after receiving his gallantry medal, and
while he was still in military service, on 29 December
1859, aged 32, at Newbridge, County Kildare, Ireland.
He was buried in an unmarked common grave at
Newbridge Cemetery. His medals are with the Royal
Scots Dragoon Guards Regimental Museum housed in
Edinburgh Castle.

JAMES MOUAT was born on 14 April 1815, at Chatham in Kent, the son of Surgeon
James Mouat, who had served with a number of infantry and cavalry regiments during
his career. His uncle had given distinguished service with the Indian Civil Medical
Service. He was educated at the University College and Hospital in London, from where
he became a Member of the Royal College of Surgeons in 1837, becoming a Fellow

in 1842. He joined the 44th (Essex) Regiment on 14
December 1838. He transferred to the 4th Regiment in
1839, and the 9th Regiment in 1848.

He became attached to the 6th Inniskilling Dragoons
on 15 August 1854, for medical service, and he was also
put in charge of the field hospital of the 3rd Division until
the fall of Sebastopol. He was the first medical man to be
awarded the Victoria Cross, being promoted Surgeon-
Major on 9 February 1855. He also received the Crimea
Medal with *Balaclava, Inkerman* and *Sebastopol* clasps,
and he was appointed to the French Legion of Honour,
and was became Commander of the Bath in 1856. He
was appointed deputy Inspector General of Hospitals on
1 October 1858.

He went on active service in New Zealand in 1861
and served throughout the Maori Wars until 1865.
During this campaign the British troops had to locate
and attack temporary wooden fortresses called Pahs,

James Mouat VC.

during which they received many casualties. He received the thanks of the New Zealand
Government for the special and very valuable service he rendered to the colony.

Surgeon-Major Mouat retired from service in 1876. Palace Garden Terrace at
Kensington in London seems to be a place to where several ex-military doctors retired,
and James lived at number 108 with his wife, Adela, from at least the time of the 1881
census. They had four servants including a coachman. He became Honorary Surgeon
to Queen Victoria in 1888, and he was appointed Knight Commander of the Order of
the Bath in 1894. Having been known throughout his life for his smart appearance,
James died at his residence on 4 January 1899, aged 83. He was buried in Kensal
Green Cemetery, where there is a memorial at his grave. His medals are with the Royal
Army Medical Corps Museum at Aldershot.

SAMUEL PARKES was born on 6 September 1815, in Wigginton, near Tamworth in
Staffordshire, and he was baptised at St Editha's Church, Tamworth, on 24 December
1815. He was the son of Thomas and Lydia Parkes, and had at least two sisters,
Elizabeth, who was baptised in 1812, and Mary, who was baptised in 1819.

He had been a general worker when he joined the 4th Light Dragoons on 28 July
1831. He was described as six feet two inches tall with a powerful frame. 635 Private
Parkes took part in the Afghanistan campaign of 1839 and for his services he was
awarded the Afghanistan Medal with *Ghuznee* clasp, for his part in the storming of
the fortress of the same name. He had been confined in cells in Ireland in 1848, being
convicted and sentenced by a district Court Martial to 56 days in Galway Prison.
His fourth and final Good Conduct badge was awarded on 18 November 1857. The

cavalry required 20 years of 'irreproachable character', which is probably why he never received the Long Service Good Conduct Medal.

Samuel was the oldest man to gain the Victoria Cross for the Crimean campaign and the citation was among the first to be announced in the London Gazette. He also received the Crimean Medal with *Alma, Balaclava* and *Sebastopol* clasps.

He was discharged on 1 December 1857, becoming a warder at Hampton Court Palace, and a Chelsea out-pensioner. He married Ann Jeffrey on 13 February 1858, at St George's Church, Hanover Square, London. By the spring of 1861 they were living at West Lodge, Marble Arch, London, where Sam was employed as a Hyde Park Constable.

He lost his original Victoria Cross and a duplicate was issued. Eventually the original turned up and was purchased by the officers of the 4th Light Dragoons and presented to the regiment on Balaclava Day 1954. The duplicate was destroyed.

Sam suffered a stroke and died on 14 November 1864, at Stanhope Lodge in Hyde Park, apparently penniless. The official cause of death was recorded as 'apoplexy – five days.' He was buried in a paupers' grave at Brompton Cemetery in west London (grave 39265). A memorial stone was laid on his grave in 1999 and a plaque was placed in St Editha's Church in Tamworth, on the 150th anniversary in 2004. The impressive medals awarded to Private Parkes are now on display at the Regimental Headquarters of the Queen's Royal Irish Hussars.

JOSEPH MALONE was born at Eccles, near Manchester, on 11 January 1833. His father was of Irish descent, and was probably one of the hundreds of labourers, or 'navvies', drafted into the area to work on the Liverpool and Manchester Railway for the engineer George Stephenson.

Joseph left his job as a farrier to enlist into the 13th Light Dragoons at Hulme

Barracks in Manchester on 28 March 1851. He was five feet seven inches tall. The regiment was stationed in Birmingham when it received orders for active service with the Light Brigade of cavalry in the Crimea. They embarked at Portsmouth in May 1854. He was promoted corporal on 14 October 1854, being promoted sergeant on 20 September 1855. For his service he received the Crimean Medal with *Alma, Balaclava, Inkerman* and *Sebastopol* clasps, issued 7 October 1855, and the Turkish Medal. His VC award was Gazetted on 25 September 1857, and he was presented with the medal by Queen Victoria at a ceremony held in the

Joseph Malone VC.

Quadrangle of Windsor Castle on 28 November 1857, with the whole of the Windsor garrison attending.

He was sent to the riding establishment at the Maidstone cavalry depot on 10 August 1857, where he remained until 10 June 1858. He was posted to Dublin, but, described as 'a very intelligent man', it was decided that he would make an efficient Riding Master. He qualified to serve with the 6th Dragoons in India and on being sent back to Maidstone, he embarked for India with the Inniskillings, being gazetted into that regiment as 450 Riding Master Malone, on 7 September 1858. He and his father-in-law, Captain Weir, were concerned with giving evidence in the court martial of Paymaster Smales of the Inniskillings at Mhow in 1861 He held the post of Assistant-Paymaster whilst this was in progress, a position which he apparently did not like. He returned from India on 6 April 1867.

He married Eliza Weir, at Mhow, India, on 3 May 1860. She was the second daughter of Captain Archibald Weir of the 6th Dragoons. There were seven children. Kate Isabella Upton was born at Ahmenugger, India, on 11 March 1861 and Joseph Archibald Edwin was born at Mhow, India, on 4 January 1863, Ada Bertha was born at Manchester on 4 July 1868, Edward Joseph was born at Brighton on 17 September 1871, Archibald Weir was born at Cahir on 26 December 1872, Eva Josephine was born at Dundalk on 1 June 1875 and Arthur Philip was born at Edinburgh on 26 February 1875. The 1881 Census shows Joseph Malone as being at the Royal Artillery Barracks, Cheriton, Kent, with his family. He attended the first Balaclava reunion banquet in 1875, and was a member of the Balaclava Commemoration Society in 1879.

He was serving at the Canterbury Cavalry Depot when orders were received for active service in South Africa, where a Boer uprising was causing serious problems, and he and his unit embarked at Chatham on 7 November 1882. While he was at the Cape he began to suffer ill health, but he had only one year of service to complete and he would not be invalided home.

Joseph died suddenly of bronchitis on 28 June 1883 in the Officers Mess at the Rugby Hotel at Pinetown, Natal, aged 50. He was buried in St Andrew's Old Cemetery, King's Road, also known as Christ's Church, Pinetown, Natal. His name is recorded on a brass tablet in Pietermaritzburg Cathedral. At the time of his death he was described as: 'an excellent, energetic, and hard-working officer'.

His medals came up for auction in June 1972 and were bought by the 13th/18th Hussars for their Regimental Museum at Cawthorne in Yorkshire. A replacement Victoria Cross was apparently authorised by the War Office in 1950 and was presented to his great-niece, Florence Malone. Hancocks confirmed in 1999 that the cross was a genuine issue by them, but not the same medal as the one presented in 1857. It was in a private collection in Australia in 2000. The centenary of the Battle of Balaclava was commemorated by a wreath-laying ceremony at his renovated grave.

His son, Joseph, known as Captain Malone, was a respected theatre director in the

West End of London during the early years of the nineteenth century, and his great-granddaughter, Sally Ann Howes, was an actress, best known as Truly Scrumptious in the film *Chitty Chitty Bang Bang*.

ALEXANDER ROBERTS DUNN was born on 15 September 1833, 'in an old-fashioned mansion' in Catherine Street, Dunstable, York, (now Toronto), which his father had built when newly arrived in Canada from England in 1820. He was the second son of John Henry Dunn, who served as receiver-general of Upper Canada from his arrival in the country until 1841 and represented Toronto in the first Canadian Parliament from 1841 to 1844. His mother was Charlotte Roberts; he was given her maiden name as his middle name. Alexander was educated at Upper Canada College and at Harrow School in England. Although only an average student, he was a keen sportsman and a good horse rider, becoming a formidable swordsman and a good marksman. Said to be an impressive-looking man, standing six feet two inches tall, he was known to have an easy-going nature.

On the death of his mother, his father moved back to England, and Alexander was commissioned as cornet in the 11th (Prince Albert's Own) Hussars, on 12 March 1852, being promoted Lieutenant on 18 February 1853. He had been away on leave when his regiment received orders for active service and purposely returned to his unit in time to sail to war with them.

A relationship developed between him and Rosa Maria Douglas, the wife of his commanding officer, who eventually asked her husband for a divorce. From then on Alexander's status in the regiment suffered and he was overlooked for a number of promotions. A troop-leader's vacancy he had applied for was given to a man who had not taken part in the Light Brigade action. He received the medal from Queen Victoria at the first investiture at Hyde Park in 1857. He also received the Crimea Medal with *Alma, Balaclava, Inkerman* and *Sebastopol* clasps, and the Turkish Medal.

He helped to raise a body of men named the Royal Canadians, who were incorporated into the British Army as the 100th Regiment (Prince of Wales's Royal Canadians), to serve in India. He was appointed Major of the regiment on 29 June 1858, and took over command while they were stationed at Aldershot. He was appointed Lieutenant-Colonel on 25 June 1861, aged only 27, and when the unit was posted to Malta in 1864, he became the youngest Colonel in

Alexander Roberts Dunn VC.

the British Army. Whilst on the island his brother, John, who was a subaltern in the regiment, died of fever, leaving Alexander as the sole heir to the family estate.

Sadness at the death of his brother and the inactivity of garrison duty prompted Colonel Dunn to seek a transfer and he became a Lieutenant-Colonel in the 33rd Regiment (Duke of Wellington's Own), station at Poona in India. He became known as a strict disciplinarian, and one of the most popular and respected officers of his day.

In late 1867 the 33rd Regiment were ordered for active service with the Abyssinian Expeditionary Force under General Napier, being sent to repatriate a number of diplomats who were being held against their will by the defiant King Theodore. Colonel Dunn is said to have had premonitions of death. During the advance into Abyssinia the force stopped at Senafe. On 25 January 1868, Colonel Dunn set off on a hunting trip with the regimental surgeon and two orderlies. Eventually the officers were separated and when Dunn and his companion stopped to take a drink, a freak accident occurred. He is believed to have caught his gaiter on the trigger of his rifle, causing it to go off, and the bullet tore into his chest and killed him. He was aged 34. He was buried with military honours in a small cemetery on high ground, which men of the regiment constructed in Senafe, now in Eritrea. A friend writing to his sister stated: 'In no regiment was ever a commanding officer so missed as the one we have so unhappily lost. So perfect a soldier, so fine a gentleman, so confidence-inspiring a leader. He was a friend, and felt to be such by every man in the regiment. The regiment will never again have so universally esteemed a commander.'

A court of enquiry was unsure about the circumstances surrounding his death and came to the supposition that it was accidental. However, it has been said that he was killed by his servant, who is believed to have confessed to the crime on his death bed in a Liverpool workhouse.

The grave site fell into disrepair, until it was rediscovered and restored and it is now under the protective eye of the Commonwealth War Graves Commission. A commemorative plaque was placed close to his family home in Toronto in 1966 and a plaque was placed in Clarence Square Park, at Spadina, Toronto. There is also a 33rd Regiment memorial at York Minster. His medals are in the possession of Upper Canada College.

JOHN BERRYMAN was born on 18 July 1825, and was baptised on 28 August, in Dudley, which at that time was in the county of Worcestershire. He was the son of Edward Berryman, a licensed victualler and proprietor of the Bell Inn. His wife Elizabeth, known as Betsy, came from Truro in Cornwall. The Bell Inn still exists in Upper High Street, opposite Dudley Town Hall. Cholera was prevalent at that time and claimed the lives of John's two brothers and a sister in 1832. In or before 1841 his father died and Betsy lived with her three surviving sons at New Mill Street in Dudley. Edmund was a puddler (ironworker), Richard a carpenter and John had begun his working life as a

John Beryman VC.

cabinet maker.

On 18 October 1843, John travelled to Birmingham to enlist into the 17th Lancers, which was the beginning of a 40-year career in the British Army. He was promoted corporal on 21 October 1851, and in early 1854 he was 'on recruitment' at Penrith in Cumbria, from 1 January to 28 February. He received orders for active service in the Crimea and when Sergeant Patrick Brennan 'drowned in the reservoir at Yenibazar' on 1 August, John was promoted to sergeant on the following day. He was present at the Battle of the Alma on 20 September 1854 and he captured three Russians in a rearguard incident at Mackenzie's Farm. Sergeant Berryman recalled his experiences for the *Strand Magazine* in 1891. Sergeant Berryman took part in night raids on Russian outposts around Sebastopol on 19 February 1855, and he left the Crimea in April 1856, being appointed Troop Sergeant-Major on 18 April 1856. For his service in the East he received the Crimea Medal with *Alma, Balaclava, Inkerman* and *Sebastopol* clasps, and the Turkish Medal.

The citation for his award of Victoria Cross states:

Served with his regiment the whole of the war, and was present at the Battle of Balaclava, where his horse being shot under him, he stopped on the field with a wounded officer amidst a shower of shot and shell. Although repeatedly told by that officer to consult his own safety and leave him, but he refused to do so, and on Sergeant Farrell coming by, with his assistance carried the officer out of range of the guns.

He received the medal from his sovereign during the first investiture at Hyde Park in 1857, becoming the eighteenth man ever to wear the Victoria Cross.

In 1857 unrest among soldiers of the Bengal Army in India flared up into rebellion, and a British force was sent to deal with it. TSM Berryman sailed with the regiment in October from Queenstown on the troopship *Great Britain*. Although they arrived at Bombay in December, they were not ready for service until May 1858, when they joined the force being prepared by Sir Hugh Rose for service in Central India. Under Sir William Gordon, they fought an extremely difficult campaign, as they pursued the leading rebel named Tantia Topi. For a distance of 1000 miles, 500 of which were covered in one month, they suffered long forced marches under the constant threat of rebel attack and the ravages of disease, after which they assaulted large, heavily-manned masonry fortresses. But they overcame these hardships and the rebel leader was captured and executed in May 1859. For his service in India he received the Indian Mutiny Medal with *Central India* clasp.

He remained in India with the regiment, where on 14 January 1861 he married Eliza Enright and they had a daughter named Florence, who was born on 21 March 1863. On 12 April 1864 he was promoted Lieutenant and Quartermaster. Sadly, as his unit were preparing to depart for England, Eliza contracted cholera and died in Bombay. John and Florence returned to England in 1865 and his daughter was initially raised by his sister, Mary, in Dudley.

The British Army invaded Zululand early in 1879 to deal with the defiant King Cetshwayo and on 22 January over 1000 British troops were massacred at Isandlwana, which sent a shock wave across the nation. Reinforcements had to be hurried out to South Africa, particularly units of cavalry. The 17th Lancers were rushed from Hounslow Barracks to the Victoria Docks, to set sail for active service at the Cape. They arrived in mid-April, and after being on escort duty with the troops, which witnessed the carnage at Isandlwana in May, they formed part of the British column that advanced on the Zulu capital at Ulundi in June. On 4 July 1879, a British force in classic square formation was attacked by a large army of Zulus and their warriors were killed in their thousands. TSM Berryman was with the Lancers who charged out of the square to finish off the enemy. The Zulu capital was destroyed and Cetshwayo was captured. For his service TSM Berryman received *the South Africa Medal* with *1879* clasp.

John attended the first Balaclava banquet, as a captain, and after the celebrations the officers dined later in the evening at Willis's Rooms in King Street. He was on the Commemoration Society lists, 1877 and 1879, described as a corporal, and he was also given the rank of corporal when he signed the Loyal Address in 1887.

He exchanged into the 5th Lancers on 19 May 1880, becoming Honorary Captain on 1 July 1881. His final promotion came on 28 July 1883, when he was appointed Honorary Major, before he retired after 40 years service. On 25 June 1886, his medals, one of the finest sets ever to be worn on the chest of a Victorian soldier, were auctioned. John and his family lived in Richmond Villa, at Langley in Buckinghamshire in early 1888 and on Balaclava Day that year he concluded the purchase of Upper Court at Woldingham in Surrey, where they lived for the rest of their lives. He was described as a farmer and retired cavalry major. For a few years he was a church warden, while his daughter, Florence, played the harmonium in church services.

Major Berryman died on 27 June 1896, aged 70, at Upper Court Farm, after a long and painful illness. In addition to the tumour there was 'secondary infection of glands in his neck, severe ulceration, haemorrhage and exhaustion.' He left a substantial amount of money to his daughter as sole executor. There was no military funeral and John was buried in the south-west corner of St Agatha's churchyard in Woldingham, where the local history society and villagers still tend his impressive pink granite gravestone.

JOHN FARRELL was born in Dublin in March 1826 and enlisted into the 17th Lancers in about 1842. He was about five feet seven inches tall. He had reached the rank of sergeant when the regiment received orders for active service in the Crimea. John Farrell carried the wounded Captain Webb 200 or so yards back to the British lines. Captain Webb had his leg amputated, 'partially under the influence of chloroform', and he died in the hospital at Scutari on 6 November 1854.

His award of the Victoria Cross was announced in the *London Gazette* on 20 November 1857 and he also received the Crimea Medal with *Alma, Balaclava, Inkerman* and *Sebastopol* clasps. He was appointed Troop Sergeant-Major on 2 May 1856 and later achieved the rank of Quartermaster-Sergeant.

QMS Farrell sailed with the regiment from Queenstown, Ireland, in October 1854, for active service in the Indian Mutiny. They were ready for service in May 1858, when they joined the force under Sir Hugh Rose which went in pursuit of the leading rebel named Tantia Topi, across Central India. They fought an extremely difficult campaign but the rebel leader was captured and executed in May 1859. For his service he received the Indian Mutiny Medal with *Central India* clasp.

The regiment were due to return home when he took ill and died from an abscess of the liver at Secunderabad, India, on 31 August 1865, aged 39. He was buried in Secunderabad Cemetery; the grave has no memorial stone.

CHARLES WOODEN was born in Germany on 24 March 1827. Nothing is known of his early life. It has been suggested that he was born in London of German parentage. He enlisted into the 17th Lancers in about 1845, becoming a Sergeant-Major.

Charles Wooden VC.

Sergeant Wooden was something of a character in the 17th Lancers. One night, returning to camp the worse for wear after a drinking session, he was challenged by the sentry on guard duty, but could not remember the password. 'Tish me', Wooden whispered in a slurred voice. 'Who?' asked the sentry, 'Tish me, Tish me!' came the answer. Down came the sentry's lance as he demanded to know just which 'me' it was. By now in a temper, Wooden bellowed: 'Tish me, the Devil.' The sentry, now exercising his better judgement on recognising his Sergeant retorted: 'Pass, Tish me the Devil!' The nickname stuck and for the remainder of his service Wooden was referred to as: 'Tish me the Devil.'

For his service in the East Sergeant-Major Wooden also received the Crimea Medal with *Alma, Balaclava, Inkerman* and *Sebastopol* clasps, the Turkish Medal, and the French War Medal. For his service in India he received the Indian Mutiny Medal with *Central India* clasp.

He exchanged into the 6th Inniskilling Dragoons, being promoted Lieutenant and Quartermaster on 26 October 1860. During his service with the Inniskillings he appeared as a witness in the court martial of a fellow officer at Aldershot in 1863. He exchanged to the 5th Lancers on 21 March 1865, and then into the 104th Bengal Fusiliers on 4 February 1871.

Charles lived on the Dover Heights in Kent, and on 23 April 1875, he complained of severe pains in his head. His wife, Eliza, sent for an army doctor, who found him in a drunken state and bleeding from his mouth and nose. Wooden pointed to his mouth and was attempting to dislodge an object, stating that he had a tooth that needed removing. The doctor examined him, and discovered that the roof of his mouth was severely damaged. There were two cartridge cases and a Colt pistol lying near him. The doctor attended to him until he died early next morning, St George's Day. It seemed that he had killed himself accidently while trying to shoot out an aching tooth. He was aged 47. He was buried at St James's Cemetery in Dover, and a headstone was erected by his brother officers, which has since been renovated (section KG grave 8-C). His medals are with the Queen's Royal Lancers Museum, at Belvoir Castle near Grantham.

No men of the 8th Hussars received the VC for action at Balaclava but five went on to gain the award for the cavalry charge at Gwalior on 17 June 1858 and operations around that region during the Indian Mutiny, which broke out in May 1857. They were Lieutenant Clement Walker Heneage, Sergeant Joseph Ward, Farrier George Hollis, and Privates John Pearson and James Champion. Surgeon Anthony Dickson Home was the doctor with the 8th Hussars at Balaclava who went on to gain the VC with the 90th Light Infantry during the first relief of Lucknow in September 1857. Seven men of the 93rd Highlanders also gained the VC, during the second relief of Lucknow in November 1857, and operations in the Lucknow region in 1858, most of whom were present in the 'Thin Red Line' at Balaclava. Only the first two named are doubtful. They were Captain William George Drummond Stewart, Lieutenant William McBean, Colour-Sergeant James Munro, Sergeant John Paton, and Privates John Dunlay, Peter Grant and David MacKay.

Distinguished Conduct Medal and Other Awards
At the commencement of the Crimean War there was no provision for an award for a particular act, or acts, of gallantry for corporals or privates, while for sergeants

the Meritorious Service Medal was of indeterminate status and could be given either for general conduct or for a particular act. This carried an annuity not exceeding £20. With this in mind, The Distinguished Conduct Medal was introduced by a Royal Warrant dated 4 December 1854, to recognise gallantry within the other ranks. The medal was the other ranks' equivalent of the Distinguished Service Order, when awarded for bravery to commissioned officers, although it ranked below that order in precedence. It was considered to be the army's second ranking gallantry award and was almost always seen as 'a near miss' for the VC. The Warrant stated:

> One Sergeant in each regiment of cavalry ... serving in the East, in the Crimea or elsewhere, shall be selected by the Commanding Officer and recommended to us for the grant of an annuity not exceeding £20. The Annuity so granted is to be at the disposal of such sergeant although he may still be in service. The sergeant to be selected for the annuity is to be the individual whom you may consider most deserving of such a reward ...

A further proposal was made in the same Warrant to extend the provisions and recommended: 'One sergeant, two corporals and four privates, to receive a medal and gratuity, this to be in the instance of a sergeant, £15, for a corporal £10 and for private £5.'The gratuity was deposited in the regimental savings bank until the recipient was discharged from service. The Warrant also stated:

> I am further directed to observe that in selecting individuals for the gratuities to be awarded for Distinguished Service or Gallant Conduct in the Field, you are not to be fettered in your selection by any consideration as to the length of service, the general good conduct of the individual (and especially in the late operations) being alone the qualifications to entitle him to the award.

Under these recommendations, men who were awarded the Distinguished Conduct Medal for the Light Brigade action at Balaclava are as follows:

4th Light Dragoons
1230 Sergeant Frederick Short, 1447 Corporal James Salamander Devlin, 1130 Corporal David John Gillam, 1452 Private William Butler, 1192 Private (saddler) Robert Ferguson, 817 Private Robert Grant and 1181 Private David Thomas.

8th Hussars
420 Regimental Sergeant-Major Samuel Williams, 453 Troop-Sergeant-Major

Michael Clarke, 1185 Corporal James Neal, 931 Private Patrick Dunn, 1153 Private William Stephen John Fulton, 934 Private Robert Moneypenny, 1078 Private Thomas Twamley and 855 Private James Whitechurch.

11th Hussars
766 Sergeant-Major George Loy Smith, 1102 Sergeant John Breeze, 1415 Sergeant John Lawson, 1564 Private James Glanister, 1337 Private Robert Martin, 709 Private Luke Oakley and 1463 Private Richard Albert Young.

13th Light Dragoons
1230 Sergeant John Mulcahey, 1199 Corporal John Allen, 1123 Corporal Matthew Long, 1363 Private John Keeley, 1529 Private John Keen, 1224 Private Joseph Moore and 984 Private Richard Rowley.

17th Lancers
483 Troop-Sergeant-Major William George Cattermole, 1168 Corporal John Penn, 405 Corporal George Taylor, 957 Private John Bowen, 1015 Private Thomas Mason, 1003 or 1214 Private George Smith and 598 Private John Vahey (or Fahey).

The Sardinian *Medaglia al Valore Militare* was issued by the Sultan of Turkey to the Allied forces of Britain, France and Sardinia who served with distinction during the Crimean campaign. Men of the Light Brigade who received it were:

4th Light Dragoons
Colonel Lord George Augustus Frederick Paget, Lieutenant-Colonel Alexander Lowe, Major Robert Portal and 1215 Troop Sergeant-Major William Waterson.

8th Hussars
Lieutenant-Colonel Rodolph de Salis, Major Edward Tomkinson and 1204 Trumpeter William Wilson.

11th Hussars
Lieutenant and Adjutant John Yates and 1495 Sergeant Robert Davis.

13th Light Dragoons
Captain Percy Shawe Smith and 1405 Corporal William Gardiner.

17th Lancers
Colonel John Lawrenson, Cornet James Duncan and 493 Troop Sergeant-Major Abraham Ranson.

Was there a Charge of the Light Brigade?

The subject of who sounded the Charge of the Light Brigade, if it was sounded at all, has been a matter of controversy since that day of blood, confusion and courage. Trumpeter Joseph Keates, 11th Hussars, was said to have sounded the charge, and the bugle he carried at Balaclava has been preserved by the regiment. On the death of Henry Joy, his troop leader, Sir George Wombwell, sent a message of sympathy to his funeral, in which he stated that he 'heard him sound the order for the charge'. The bugle of Trumpeter William Brittain, 17th Lancers, who was Orderly-Trumpeter to Lord Cardigan at Balaclava, came up for auction in 1964 as 'The bugle which sounded the Charge of the Light Brigade'. It was presented to the 17th/21st Lancers Museum. A third trooper of the 17th Lancers, Trumpeter Martin Lanfried, spoke on BBC Radio, and blew the bugle on which he said he had 'sounded the Charge of the Light Brigade.' A further twist to the controversy was provided by the late Canon William Lummis, who was an authority on the subject and actually knew some of the survivors. He was of the opinion that the charge was never sounded. He believed that Trumpeter Joy sounded the charge of the Heavy Brigade.

The Commanders in Later Life

Of the commanding officers who led their men with such great gallantry at Balaclava, only one reached the age of 70. As has been stated, Captain Oldham was killed during the Light Brigade action. Colonel Shewell's constitution eventually broke down and he went home on sick leave. He died at Gosden near Guildford in 1856, aged 47. Captain Morris died while on active service during the mutiny in India in 1858, apparently from the effects of the sun on the metal plate he had attached to his skull to fix and protect the head wound he had suffered at Balaclava. He was aged 37. Lord Cardigan spent much of the rest of his life trying to justify his behaviour during the Light Brigade action. His aristocratic background and particular upbringing gave him an air of stubborn pomposity, but as one supporter stated: 'It is only wasting words to doubt his bravery.' He retired from public life in 1866 and died in 1868, aged 70, after falling from a horse in the grounds of his estates at Deene Park in Northamptonshire. Colonel Douglas became the victim of a scandal when his wife ran away with Lieutenant Dunn VC. He was appointed major-general in 1868, and died at Aldershot in 1871. Lord Paget came in for much criticism when he returned to England on the death of his father. He had intended to retire but was forced to return to the war zone in 1855, where he took command of the Light Brigade. He lost his Beaumaris seat in 1857. He commanded a division of the Bengal Army in India from 1862 to 1865 and became inspector-general of cavalry on his return to England. He was made KCB in 1870 and died suddenly at his Mayfair residency in 1880, aged 62.

In Memoriam

There are some memorials around the country dedicated to officers who were killed at Balaclava. Among them is one to Captain George Lockwood in St Mary's Church at Lambourne in Essex, which states: 'Every effort to recover his remains having been proved ineffectual this monument is erected by his mother as a tribute of love to an affectionate and dutiful son.' There is a memorial at Newstead Abbey in Nottinghamshire dedicated to Captain Alexander Webb by his brother, William Frederick Webb. There is a plaque in the Harrow School Chapel dedicated to Hugh Montgomery and a stained glass window in St Patrick's Church at Drumbeg near Belfast.

Alfred, Lord Tennyson brought the Light Brigade action at Balaclava to the attention of the British public in his celebrated poem *The Charge of the Light Brigade*, which he began to pen almost as soon as the incident was brought to his notice. It was published in the *Examiner* on 9 December 1854. On 25 October 1875, survivors of the Battle of Balaclava attended a reunion banquet held at the Alexandra Palace in London. Veterans who had taken part in the Light Brigade action were interviewed for the *Illustrated London News*, and it was found that some had become in-pensioners at the Chelsea Hospital, while many more had fallen on hard times. It was decided to form a Balaclava Commemoration Society, which came into being in 1877; in 1879 the society restricted its members to those who had taken part in the Light Brigade action at Balaclava. On the occasion of Queen Victoria's Golden Jubilee in 1887, the survivors signed a Loyal Address which was presented to her.

In 1890 some of the survivors were living in poverty and many were in the workhouse. Even that great champion of the underdog – the British public – seemed to have forgotten them. A public appeal for funds to help them raised just £24. Rudyard Kipling responded with a sardonic verse: 'There were thirty million English who talked of England's might/There were twenty broken troopers who lacked a bed for the night.' (See page ***) Some of the contents were fanciful, but the words rang true and he highlighted the plight of many Light Brigade veterans in his *The Last of the Light Brigade*, published in the *St James's Gazette* of 28 April 1890. The national conscience was finally pricked. The *St James's Gazette* set up the Light Brigade Relief Fund in the following month.

On 30 July 1890, Tennyson, Florence Nightingale and Martin Lanfried, who had been a 17th Lancers bugler during the Charge, were enlisted to make supportive phonograph recordings. Suddenly, the old boys were celebrities, taking bows before cheering theatre audiences at benefit concerts in Manchester and other cities and towns across the country. They even lined up in Buffalo Bill's Wild West show. On 25

October 1890 a dinner was held at the Alexandra Palace, and these continued on the anniversary of the battle until 1913, by which time there were few survivors left.

In 1895, as the result of an article appearing in *Illustrated Bits*, a periodical published from the offices of T. Harrison Roberts in Fleet Street, London, Mr Roberts became interested in the lives of the Light Brigade men and he was concerned to learn that many of them lived in poverty. He was a generous philanthropist and he decided to start a public fund, begun in July 1897. Survivors received a weekly pension from the fund and no recipient of the T.H. Roberts Relief Fund needed to enter a workhouse or have a pauper's burial. In the same year he invited 73 survivors to an all-expenses-paid visit to his offices in Fleet Street to watch Queen Victoria's Diamond Jubilee procession on 22 June. The sovereign stopped her carriage to acknowledge the party of proud veterans. Survivors received a weekly pension from the fund. A few survivors were too proud to claim financial help from the fund, but pride does not fill a family's stomachs, and the fund brought immediate relief to about 40 men.

Even some of the horses received worthy recognition. Lieutenant-Colonel de Salis was so impressed by the bravery and stamina of his wounded horse, 'Drummer Boy' he decided that he deserved an award as much as the men. He acquired a Crimea campaign medal and had the rim engraved with the horse's name and the fact that he had been born in Ireland in 1848. Of the 112 horses that carried men of the 13th Light Dragoons into battle at Balaclava, only one returned to England. The horse was called 'Butcher' because of the number and severity of the wounds he received during the action. This horse was presented to Queen Victoria when the 13th Light Dragoons embarked for India in 1874 and was kept at Hampton Court until his death in about 1881, when he must have been over 30 years old. The stallion named 'Old Bob' that carried Farrier-Major Charles Avison, 11th Hussars, into the Valley of Death, and had also been present at the Alma and Inkerman, became a legend. He was re-named 'Crimean Bob' and, having never had a day's sickness, on his death at the age of 34 while still in service at Cahir, Ireland, in 1862, he was given a military funeral and a tombstone was erected to his memory.

Lord Cardigan's horse 'Ronald', a chestnut with white socks standing 15.2 hands high, had been bred by the Earl at Deene Park. The horse's last service to his master was to follow the coffin in his funeral cortege. However, he became boisterous, so to avoid the solemn day being ruined by the over-excited horse they administered laudanum. This turned out to be a disaster when no one could move the dozing charger. Eventually an inspired individual called for the sounding of the cavalry charge, which stirred Ronald into life and he set off as required. Ronald died on 28 June 1872, and the Brudenell family honoured the valiant old horse by preserving his tail and his head in the White Hall at the family country seat in Northamptonshire. One of his hooves was placed on a bronze pillow surmounted by a statue of Lord Cardigan riding him. This can be seen today at The King's Royal Hussars Museum.

The dog Jemmy returned to England with the regiment, and at Dundalk Colonel de

Salis had a special collar made for him, to which four clasps were attached for service at *Alma, Balaclava, Inkerman* and *Sebastopol,* which he wore on special parade days. He embarked with the regiment for India and marched with it daily until after the action on 14 August 1858. While attempting to swim across the Chambal River in the following month he was swept away and drowned. The body was recovered and a clasp for *Central India* was added to the collar, which is kept on display at the Officers' Mess.

The Light Brigade action at Balaclava was ill-fated before it began, and had little effect on the outcome of the battle. However, it had a devastating effect on the enemy's mounted units, who were reluctant to face British cavalry for the rest of the conflict. Contrary to popular belief, the men who took part were proud of what they had achieved, and some stated that they would have done it again had they been ordered to do so. It is still considered by many military enthusiasts to be, as Lord Raglan stated: 'The finest thing ever done'. Edwin Hughes is quoted as saying:

> You never think of honours or glory at the time, but I am proud now that I was in the Charge. There was death all around us, but it was a glorious affair, and I have never regretted that I was there.

The memory of what it was actually like to have taken part in the Light Brigade action at Balaclava died with him in 1927.

SKETCHES OF THE LIGHT BRIGADE

The Charge of the Light Brigade

Alfred, Lord Tennyson

Half a league, half a league,
Half a league onward,
All in the Valley of Death
Rode the Six Hundred.
'Forward, the Light Brigade!
Charge for the guns!' he said,
Into the Valley of Death
Rode the Six Hundred.

'Forward, the Light Brigade!'
Was there a man dismayed?
Not though the soldier knew
Some one had blundered;
Theirs not to make reply,
Theirs not to reason why,
Theirs but to do and die;
Into the Valley of Death
Rode the Six Hundred.

Cannon to right of them,
Cannon to left of them,
Cannon in front of them
Volleyed and thundered;
Stormed at with shot and shell,
Boldly they rode and well,
Into the jaws of Death,
Into the mouth of Hell
Rode the Six Hundred.

Flashed all their sabres bare,
Flashed as they rode in air,
Sabring the gunners there,
Charging an army, while
All the world wondered;
Plunged in the battery smoke
Right through the line they broke,
Cossack and Russian
Reeled from the sabre-stroke,
Shattered and sundered.
Then they rode back, but not,
Not the Six Hundred.

Cannon to right of them,
Cannon to left of them,
Cannon behind them
Volleyed and thundered.
Stormed at with shot and shell,
While horses and hero fell,
They that had fought so well
Came through the jaws of Death
Back from the mouth of Hell,
All that was left of them,
Left of Six Hundred.

When can their glory fade?
Oh! The wild charge they made!
All the world wondered;
Honour the charge they made,
Honour the Light Brigade,
Noble Six Hundred.

The Last of the Light Brigade

Rudyard Kipling

There were thirty million English, who talked of England's might,
There were twenty broken troopers who lacked a bed for the night.
They had neither food nor money, they had neither service nor trade,
They were only shiftless soldiers, the last of the Light Brigade.

They felt that life was fleeting, they knew not that art was long,
That though they were dying of famine, they lived in deathless song.
They asked for little money to keep the wolf from the door,
And the thirty million English sent twenty pounds and four!

They laid their heads together that were scarred and lined and grey,
Keen were the Russian sabres, but want was keener than they.
And an old Troop-Sergeant muttered, 'Let us go to the man who writes,
The things on Balaclava the kiddies at school recites.'

They went without bands or colours, a regiment ten-file strong,
To look for the Master-singer who had crowned them all in his song.
And, waiting his servant's order, by the garden gate they stayed,
A desolate little cluster, the last of the Light Brigade.

They strove to stand to attention, to straighten the toil-bowed back,
They drilled on an empty stomach, the loose-knit files fell slack.
With stooping of weary shoulders, in garments tattered and frayed,
The shambled in his presence, the last of the Light Brigade.

The old Troop-Sergeant was spokesman, and 'Beggin' your pardon,' he said,
'You wrote o' the Light Brigade, sir. Here's all that isn't dead.'
An' it's all come true what you wrote, sir, regardin' the mouth of hell,
For we're all us nigh in the workhouse, an' we thought we'd call an' tell.

No thank you we don't want food, sir, but couldn't you take an write,
A sort of 'to be continued' and 'see next page' of the fight?
We think that someone has blundered, an' couldn't you tell 'em how?
You wrote we were heroes once, sir. Please, write we are starving now.'

The poor little army departed, limping and lean and forlorn,
And the heart of the Master-singer grew hot with 'the scorn of the scorn.'

And he wrote for them wonderful verses that swept the land like flame,
'Till the fatted souls of the English were scourged with the thing called Shame.

O thirty million English that babble of England's might,
Behold there are twenty heroes who lack their food tonight.'
Our children's children are lisping to 'honour the charge they made –'
And we leave to the streets and the workhouse, the charge of the Light Brigade!'

David Andrews was born at Maidenhead in 1831, and he entered the 11th Hussars in 1841. On his discharge from the army he settled in Gorton, Manchester, where he died in 1884, aged 52. He was buried at Weaste Cemetery in Salford.

William Bentley was born at Kilnwick-on-the-Wolds in Yorkshire, on 25 October 1816, a date which was to have great significance on his life. He came from a farming family, and some of his descendants still farm in the Yorkshire dales. He enlisted into the 11th Hussars in 1835, and he was on duty with the troops who escorted Prince Albert to London for his marriage to Queen Victoria. He took part in the Light Brigade action at Balaclava on his 38th birthday. He was promoted to Sergeant-Major in 1855, and discharged from the army in 1860. His intended place of residence was given as the Royal Wiltshire Yeomanry at Calne, and he served with that unit as drill instructor for twelve years. When he retired in 1884 he had been in military service for 37 years. William died at his home in York in 1891, after a long illness. He was aged 74, and he was buried with military honours at York Cemetery. Fellow chargers John Hogan and William Pearson attended the funeral.

Seth Bond was born in the village of Frant, near Tunbridge Wells, Kent, in 1822. When he was sixteen years old he joined the 35th (Royal Sussex) Regiment, before transferring to the 11th Hussars in 1840. He was promoted Troop Sergeant Major in 1857 and retired from the army in 1864. He settled in Southam, Warwickshire, where he became landlord of the Harp Inn. He was attached to the Repton and Gresley Yeomanry in 1865, eventually becoming a farmer. Seth died in 1902, aged 80, and he was buried in Southam.

Richard Brown was born at Wrighton in Yorkshire, in 1825. He worked as a rural labourer until he enlisted into the 11th Hussars in 1843. He was described as: 'Handsome and honest, he was truly a model soldier, for, in his long service of 21 years he was never in the defaulters' book. It was said that if he had not been illiterate he would have 'borne Her Majesty's commission'. He suffered with rheumatism and after receiving a severe rupture he discharged in 1864 to become a horse dealer in York. He moved across the Pennines to Manchester and became a riding master in Fallowfield. It was reported in 1902 that: 'For twelve years subsequent to his retirement from the service he worked (often knee-deep in water) at a canal side in Manchester, but when age and rheumatism rendered him incapable, he was compelled to go to the workhouse.' He was living in lodgings in Hulme when he was admitted to the Union Workhouse at Withington, where he died in 1890, aged 65. He was buried in Philips Park Cemetery, Manchester.

John Charles Buckton was born in London in 1827 and enlisted into the 11th Hussars in 1848. He left the army in 1861 and worked as a viewer at the Government clothing store in Pimlico. He died in London in 1906, aged 68.

William Butler was born at Ormskirk in 1825, and was brought up in Preston. He was a shoemaker prior to joining the 17th Lancers in 1846. He was on parade at the Great Exhibition in Hyde Park in 1851, and in the following year he was present at the funeral of the Duke of Wellington. He was appointed master bootmaker and sergeant in the 18th Regiment, before taking his final discharge in 1867. He started a business in London, but he eventually returned to Preston, where worked as a shoemaker at Black Horse Yard, Preston, before moving to Blackpool. William died in 1901, aged 75, and he was buried in Layton Cemetery, Blackpool.

James Cameron was born in Australia in 1813 and he was aged 13 when he joined the 13th Light Dragoons in India in 1826. Corporal Cameron was wounded at Balaclava. His injuries were exacerbated by the fact that he was sent on board ship to Scutari hospital without being attended to by a surgeon. On leaving the army, he and his wife lived with their son at the Brunswick Inn at Broughton in Salford. In 1881 a function was held at the pub to celebrate the anniversary of the Battle of Balaclava and to honour Corporal Cameron, who wore his medals and spoke about his military career. James died in 1882, aged 70, and was buried at Weaste Cemetery, Salford.

Dennis Connor enlisted into the 4th Light Dragoons in 1841 and discharged in 1866. He attended the Balaclava Reunion Banquet in 1875 and in the following year the man who had served his country for 25 years was handed over to the St Luke's Parish Authorities in London as a mental patient; he was placed in the workhouse.

Francis Dickinson was born in Sheffield in 1830. He enlisted as a 16-year-old boy soldier into the 17th Lancers at the Old Barracks, Sheffield, on 2 May 1846. He retired from the army in 1870, after 24 years service, when the men of his troop presented him with an engraved silver goblet. He became the landlord at the Earl Grey public house in Eccleshall Road, Sheffield, where he was a prominent member of the Sheffield Crimean and Indian Mutiny Veterans Association. Francis died at Heeley, Sheffield, in 1898, aged 68, and he was buried with military honours in Sheffield General Cemetery.

Patrick Doolan was born at Nenagh, County Tipperary, Ireland, in 1825, and enlisted into the 8th Hussars at Dublin in 1846. The serious wounds he received at Balaclava had damaged several important nerves in his face and he was discharged as unfit in 1855. He died in Dublin in 1904, aged 79.

John Edden was born at Tamworth in Staffordshire in 1833. He enlisted into the 4th Light Dragoons in 1851. He discharged from the army in 1863 and returned to Tamworth, where he worked as a labourer to a stonemason. John died in 1898, aged 65. His impressive obelisk memorial can still be seen in Tamworth Cemetery at Wiggington.

John Forbes was born at Dull in Scotland in 1821. He was employed as a clerk before joining the 4th Light Dragoons in 1845, and he discharged in 1869, having served for 24 years. On moving to live in Newcastle-upon-Tyne, he became staff sergeant with the Northumberland Hussars Yeomanry Cavalry, lived at the Riding School in Bath Road, Newcastle. He had a total military service of over 37 years. John died at his home in Northumberland Road, Newcastle, in 1895, aged 76. He was buried in St Andrews Cemetery, Newcastle, with military honours provided by the Northumberland Fusiliers. His sword, busby, and medals were placed on the coffin. A wreath was placed at his grave on Armistice Day, 1954, to commemorate the centenary of the Battle of Balaclava.

Isaac Hanson was born at Ossett, near Wakefield, Yorkshire. He had worked as a shoe maker before enlisting into the 13th Light Dragoons in 1840. On his discharge in 1862, after serving nearly 22 years, he went to live in Brindle Street, Bradford. He was described as being: 'not now equal to regular work'. He had been living at Cawthorpe, near Wakefield, when he was admitted as an in-pensioner at the Royal Hospital, Chelsea, in 1873. Isaac died on the 24th anniversary of the Battle of Balaclava in 1878 and he was buried in Brompton Cemetery.

Clement Walker Heneage was born at Compton Bassett in Wiltshire in 1831. He joined the 8th Hussars in 1851 and was promoted Lieutenant while on active service in 1854. He was later awarded the Victoria Cross for his valour during a charge made by the 8th Hussars at Gwalior during the Indian Mutiny, 1858. He died at Compton Bassett in 1901, aged 70. He is buried in St Swithun's Parish Church.

Edward Hindley was born at Liverpool in 1831 and enlisted into the 13th Light Dragoons in 1853. On his discharge he lived at Princess Park, Liverpool, before moving to Wavertree. He died at his home on 21 November 1911, aged 80. He was buried with military honours in Toxteth Park Cemetery, Liverpool. There is no memorial stone. He had received help from the T H Roberts Fund, which paid his funeral expenses and supported his widow. Edward Hindley's Medals were left to Mr Roberts and were still with his family until February 1998, when they were sold at auction for over £12,000.

John Howes was born at Wymondham near Norwich in 1828 and he enlisted in the 4th Light Dragoons in 1846. He rode in the Charge as a sergeant. He retired in 1860 as Troop Sergeant Major, having completed 24 years service. He settled in Jamaica Row near Birmingham city centre, where he lived for many years. He and John Parkinson helped form the Birmingham Military Veterans Association in 1894, to aid local survivors of the Crimean and Indian Mutiny campaigns, and in the following year he was instrumental in arranging the annual dinner in Birmingham. Having moved to Edgebaston, John died on Christmas morning 1902 and he was buried with military honours at Lodge Hill Cemetery, Birmingham.

Edwin Hughes was born in Wrexham in 1830. He retired from the 13th Light Dragoons as Squadron Sergeant-Major in 1873, having served for 21 years. He was presented with a marble clock by the NCOs of the regiment. He went to live in Birmingham and served as Instructor to the Worcestershire Yeomanry for 12 years until 1886. He attended several annual dinners, including the one held in Birmingham in 1895, and the last one in 1913. He settled in Blackpool and the living memory of what it was actually like to have ridden in the immortal Charge of the Light Brigade died with him in 1927. He was buried in Layton Cemetery, Blackpool, with military honours provided by his old regiment.

Thomas George Johnson was born in 1824, at Maidstone, Kent, the youngest in a family of 11 children. His father was a clerk on the Cavalry depot staff at Maidstone, and two of his brothers were in the army. Thomas joined the 4th Light Dragoons in 1837 as a 13-year-old boy, by special authority. He transferred to the 13th Light Dragoons in 1846. He became an officer in the 13th Hussars, and retired by sale of his commission in 1869. He succeeded his brother as Adjutant of the 2nd West Yorkshire Yeomanry Cavalry at Halifax. On his retirement in 1881, Major Johnson lived in Southowram, near Halifax, before taking over as manager of the Royal Hotel in Scarborough. Major Johnson died at his residence in South Cliff, Scarborough, in 1908, aged 84, and he was buried in Dean Road Cemetery, Scarborough. There is a picture of him in the 13th/18th Hussars Museum at Cannon Hall, Barnsley, which his family descendants ironically refer to as being of 'The Czar', because of his likeness to a Russian.

Henry Joy was born at Ripon in Yorkshire in 1819. He was the son of a trooper in the 1st Life Guards who fought under The Duke of Wellington at Waterloo. Henry entered the army as a 14-year-old band boy in 1833. He was appointed trumpet-major in 1847 and was in charge of the band at the funeral of the Duke of Wellington. Having received the DCM for his service at Balaclava, he became a messenger to the Duke of Cambridge at the War Office when he left the army. Henry died at his home in Chiswick in 1893 in his 75th year and he was buried with military honours in Chiswick Old Cemetery.

John Ashley Kilvert was born near Shrewsbury in Shropshire in 1833. After being educated at High Ercall Grammar School, he worked for a wine and spirits merchant in Birmingham. The regimental headquarters of the 11th Hussars was in Nottingham by 1851 and it was there that he enlisted that year. John discharged in 1861 and set up business as a pawnbroker in Wednesbury (now in the West Midlands). He took a keen interest in the public duties of the town, being elected an alderman in 1884, and he was mayor during the period 1905–1906. John died at his home, 'Balaclava House', in 1920. He was buried with military honours in a private walled grave at Wood Green Cemetery in Wednesbury.

Alexander Low was born in Bath in 1817 and entered the 4th Light Dragoons in 1835, rising to the rank of Brevet-Major just before leaving for the Crimea. A skilled and professional cavalryman, he was promoted to major on the day after the Charge and he was appointed CB in 1867. He transferred to the 2nd Dragoon Guards in 1874 and retired as a general in 1881, being appointed to the command of the 4th Light Dragoons. He was appointed KCB in June 1904. Sir Alexander Low died in Geneva the following month.

John Linkon was born in Cambridge in 1816 and he enlisted into the 13th Light Dragoons in 1835. On his discharge from the army in 1861, he went to live in Weymouth, Dorset, where he was Drill Instructor to the Hampshire Carabiniers (Yeomanry), from 1862 to 1869. In civilian life he was an agent for the Prudential Insurance Company. John eventually settled in Portsmouth, where he died in 1910, aged 94, and he was buried in Portsea Cemetery.

Charles Macauley was born at Rawcliffe, Yorkshire, on 3 June 1828, the son of surgeon Richard Macauley. He was a tailor, living in Leeds, when he enlisted into the 6th Dragoon Guards in 1846. He transferred to the 8th Hussars in 1848. He was discharged in 1865 and returned to Leeds. He died on 5 January 1905, aged 76. He was buried at Woodhouse Cemetery. His name appears on the Crimea Memorial at Leeds Parish Church.

Robert Martin was born in London in 1828 and enlisted into the 11th Hussars in 1847. He lived in Fulham and worked at Hampton Court Palace for many years. Forced to retire through ill-health, he moved north to live at New Ferry, Wirral, becoming an active member of the New Ferry Lads Brigade. Robert died in 1900, aged 72. He was buried with military honours at Bebbington Cemetery.

Thomas Morley – 'A great, rough, bellowing Nottingham man' – was born in 1830. He had been an engineer before he enlisted into the 17th Lancers in 1849, being promoted to sergeant after the charge in 1854. 'The man of the hour' was disappointed that he did not receive a gallantry medal for his actions at Balaclava and Inkerman. He purchased his discharge in 1857 and became drill sergeant to the Sherwood Rangers Yeomanry at Mansfield. When the American Civil War began he gained a commission in the 12th Pennsylvania Volunteer Cavalry, Union Army, being taken prisoner again during the Battle of Bull Run. He spent several months in Libby Prison before being released for medical reasons. He resigned his commission as captain in 1865. Returning to Britain, he lived in Scotland and was appointed Drill Troop-Sergeant-Major in the Ayrshire Yeomanry in 1868. He returned to America in 1884, where he became Quartermaster in the United States Army and took American citizenship to work in the War Department. Returning to Nottingham, he was admitted to the Nottingham City Asylum, where he died in 1906. He was buried with full military honours in Nottingham Cemetery.

Robert Nichol was born in Coventry in 1834, where his father was stationed with the 8th Hussars. On his discharge his father took the family to settle in Newcastle-upon-Tyne. In 1843 Robert was sent away to attend the Royal Military Asylum in Chelsea. He had worked as a shoemaker prior to enlisting into the army on 25 October 1848, a date which would have great significance a few years later. Private Nichol took part in the notorious 'Bareback' reconnaissance. On leaving the army in 1856, he joined the Merchant Navy as a steward, before returning to Newcastle. He worked for the Tyne Commissioners and on one occasion he helped to paint the famous bridge. He joined Newcastle Corporation and he was the keeper of the smallpox hospital at Byker. Robert died in 1897, aged 64. He was buried in St John's Cemetery, Newcastle.

James Ikin Nunnerley was born in Warrington, (now Cheshire) in 1830. He was apprenticed to a draper before he enlisted into the 17th Lancers in 1847. In 1852 he was on escort duty for the funeral of the Duke of Wellington. On taking his discharge in 1857, he became station master on the railway at Disley near Stockport, before moving to Ormskirk in Lancashire in 1859, where he became drill instructor to D Troop in Lord Lathom's Lancashire Hussars. He retired as Sergeant-Major in 1881 and opened a drapery shop in Moor Street, Ormskirk. James died on 22 November 1905, aged 75. He was buried with military honours in Ormskirk Parish Churchyard.

John Smith Parkinson was born at Grantham in 1835 and he enlisted into the 11th Hussars in 1851. He formed a 'Corps Dramatique' within the regiment, and he acted as its stage manager. He left the army in 1864 and he was employed with the South Eastern Railway Company at London Bridge until 1866, when he left London for family health reasons. He became a mounted officer with the Birmingham Police Force, serving the greater part of his service with B Division at Ladywood, where he became a sergeant. He retired from the police force in 1892 and lived at Aston, Birmingham. He and fellow charger John Howes were foremost in establishing the Birmingham Military Veterans' Association. When the Balaclava Commemoration Society held their 1895 reunion in Birmingham, Sergeant Parkinson took a leading part in its organisation. He lived at Yardley, Birmingham, and died in 1917, aged 82. He was buried with military honours at Yardley Cemetery, Birmingham.

William Pearson was born at Doncaster in 1825, and he enlisted into the 17th Lancers in 1848. After the Battle of Balaclava he was placed under the personal care of Florence Nightingale at Scutari. He served during the Indian Mutiny, and discharged in 1860. He settled in York, where he gained employment as turnkey at York Castle prison, where he freely admitted that he gave the lash to unruly inmates. William died in 1909, aged 84. He was buried with military honours in York Cemetery.

William Pearson was born in Penrith, (now Cumbria) in 1826. He was a leather dresser before he ran away to enlist into the 4th Light Dragoons in 1848. While serving in the East, the severe Crimean winter left him with frostbite and he spent Christmas Eve 1854 having the four lesser toes amputated from his right foot, being nursed by Florence Nightingale. He was presented to Queen Victoria at Brompton Barracks on 3 March 1855. Later that year he was discharged as unfit for further military service. He became Inspecting Officer's Orderly to the Dalemain troop, Cumberland and Westmoreland Imperial Yeomanry. In 1880 he moved to Underbarrow, near Kendal, where he set up a fellmongering and tanning business at Thorns Villa. In 1906 he turned the business over to his sons and retired. He went to live in Kendal, where he died in 1909, aged 82. He was buried with military honours in Parkside Cemetery, Kendal. There is a portrait of him in Penrith Museum. In 1971 a street was named after him, a plaque was erected at his birthplace, and Penrith Council mistakenly purchased a set of medals which proved not to be his. However, in 1978 the authentic medals were located and they are now displayed in Penrith Museum.

John Penn was born in 1818, of Irish descent, being the son of Farrier-Major John Penn of the 14th Light Dragoons, who was killed by a kick from a horse when John was only eight years old. John joined the 3rd Light Dragoons, with whom he served in Afghanistan and India, and took part in several battles. He transferred to the 17th Lancers in 1853, when he heard they may be sent on active service. He retired from the regular army in 1863 and settled in the cavalry depot town of Dunbar, where he was appointed drill-sergeant with the East Lothian Yeamanry Cavalry. He died at Dunbar in 1886, aged 68. He was buried in the local churchyard.

William Purvis was born at Bridgetown, Glasgow, in 1825, and he had previously been a factory guider in Ireland before he enlisted into the 17th Lancers in 1846. He was promoted to sergeant in 1857 and he took part in the Indian Mutiny in 1858, being discharged as Troop Sergeant-Major in1870 after over 24 years service. He was drill instructor at various Yeomanry schools in Walsall, Birmingham, Cannock, Wednesbury and Birmingham, making a total of 42 years military service. William died in 1899 and he was buried at Ryecroft Cemetery in Walsall. There is a memorial tablet dedicated to him in St Matthew's Church.

John Richardson was born at Carlisle in 1827, and enlisted into the 11th Hussars in 1852. He was stationed in Manchester in 1858. When he went absent Adjutant John Yates caused him to receive 50 lashes 'in the riding school like a dog', and to be imprisoned. His father wrote to the Duke of Cambridge, who ordered him to be liberated and discharged. He was the last man flogged in Hulme Barracks. He went to America in 1863 and joined the New Jersey Volunteers, for service in the Civil War. He fought at the Battle of Pittsburg and returned home in 1865. Towards the end of his life his sight began to fail him and he was forced to enter the Crumpsall Workhouse, where he died in 1897, aged 70. He was buried with military honours at Philips Park Cemetery, Manchester. In 1988 a new memorial stone was laid at his grave.

James Scarfe was born at Rotterdale, Suffolk, in 1815. He enlisted into the 17th Lancers in 1835, being appointed saddler-sergeant in 1849. His wife gave birth to a baby daughter on the day of the Battle of Balaclava! He was among the soldiers seen by Queen Victoria at Brompton in 1855. He had ten sabre wounds to various parts of his body and his sight was severely damaged. He was admitted to the Chelsea Hospital in 1855 and later became a Yeoman of the Guard. James died in 1886, aged 70. His two sons also served with the 17th Lancers.

Edward Seager's family had lived in and around Liverpool for 200 years. Edward was born in 1812. On 29 November 1839 he became Regimental Sergeant-Major with the 8th Hussars, being promoted lieutenant in 1843. He was adjutant from 1841 until the day of the Battle of Balaclava, when he was promoted captain. He served as a major during the Indian Mutiny. He commanded the regiment for a period during the early part of 1859, being appointed Major-General in 1870. He received the Distinguished Conduct Medal in 1872. He served as Inspecting Officer of Yeomanry Cavalry at York from 1873 to 1878, being appointed CB. He retired in 1881. General Seager died in Scarborough in 1883, aged 70. He was buried in Smithdown Road Cemetery, Liverpool. His family have his medals, sword, letters, and parts of his uniform.

William Sewell was born at Dorking in 1832 and he enlisted
into the 13th Light Dragoons in 1851. He was discharged at
Chatham as unfit for further service in 1855. He had received a
severe wound to his head at Balaclava, as a result of which he
wore a metal plate fixed over the wound for the rest of his life.
He settled in Liverpool, where he became coachman to the Earl
family, and lived at Woolton Hill. William died at Mossley Hill,
Liverpool in 1910, aged 78. He was buried at St Peter's Parish
Church, Woolton, Liverpool.

George Loy Smith was born at Woolwich in 1817. He came from a military family, his grandfather having served under the Duke of York in Flanders, his father served during the Duke of Wellington's Peninsular campaign and two of his uncles fought in the service of their country. He was apprenticed to a chemist before he enlisted into the 11th Hussars in 1833 and joined the regiment in India. He is believed to have been the 'last man that returned up the valley' and he was a central figure for Lady Butler's painting 'After the Charge'. He retired in 1859 and was appointed a Yeoman of the Guard that same year, performing many civic duties in the presence of royalty and other dignitaries. George died at St Bartholomew's Hospital, London, in 1888, aged 71.

William Smith was born in 1822 and on enlisting into the 3rd Light Dragoons in 1836 he served on the North West Frontier of India. He transferred to the 11th Hussars in 1853, when he heard that they were preparing for active service in the Crimea. On his discharge he settled at Knutsford in Cheshire and in 1863 he became Trumpet-Major to the Earl of Chester's Cheshire Yeomanry, retiring in 1874. He was manager of the Knutsford Gentlemens' Club. He died in 1879, aged 57, having overdosed on laudanum, 'taken while he was in an unsound state of mind.' He was buried in Knutsford Parish Churchyard, During the Festival of Britain celebrations in 1951 a commemoration plaque was placed at his former home; there is a portrait of him in Knutsford Library and in 1989 a new memorial stone was dedicated to him.

Richard Hall Williams was born at Bath in 1821. He was a compositor by trade. When his family moved to Eccles near Manchester, he began his working life as a booking clerk at Worsley railway station, before he enlisted into the 17th Lancers in 1843. He served in the Indian Mutiny and after spending nine years in India he discharged in 1867. He became post-master at the Worsley village post office and TSM with the Worsley Troop of the Duke of Lancaster's Own Yeomanry. A 'highly respected member of the community', he worshipped at the Worsley Parish Church. He was one of the founder members of the Worsley Lodge of Freemasons, of which the Earl of Ellesmere was the first Master. Richard died in 1910, aged 91. He was buried with military honours at St Mark's Parish Church, Worsley.

Thomas Wright was born at Warrington in 1830 and he enlisted into the 17th Lancers on the day after his 21st birthday in 1851. He went on to serve in the Indian Mutiny in 1858 and he discharged from military service in 1861. He lived in Norwood, London, and became a Warden at Maidstone Prison. 'Old Tom' eventually moved back north and settled in Widnes, Cheshire. He died in 1902, aged 71. He was buried at Farnworth Cemetery in Widnes, where a Great War VC winner and two men who took part in the defence of Rorke's Drift during the Zulu War of 1879 are also buried.

BIBLIOGRAPHY

Anon, 'The Charge of the Light Brigade, By One Who Was In It' *The United Services Journal* (1856)

Adlington, Lieutenant Henry, *Letters from the Crimea* (1854–55)

Anglesey, The Marquess of, *A History of the British Cavalry* (Volume 3) (1973)

Answers Magazine, *Portraits and Accounts of 14 Survivors* (1912)

Bacon, General A., *The British Cavalry at Balaclava* (1855)

Bancroft, James W., *The Way to Glory* (1988)

_____, *Devotion to Duty* (1990)

_____, *Local Heroes: The Light Brigade at Balaclava* (2001)

_____, *Some of the Six Hundred* (2007)

_____, *More of the Six Hundred* (2010)

Barrett, Charles R.B., *History of the 13th Hussars* (2 volumes) (1911)

Berryman, Major John, account in the *Strand* magazine (1891)

Boys, E.J. *Lives of the Light Brigade* (ongoing archive)

Brett-Smith, Richard, *The 11th Hussars* (1969)

Brighton, Terry, *Hell Riders: The Truth About the Charge of the Light Brigade* (2004)

Brown, Sergeant Richard, 'How the Country Rewards Its Heroes: A Talk With One of the Six Hundred' *Manchester Guardian* (1890)

Butler, Sergeant William, *A Descriptive Account of the Famous Charge of the Light Brigade* (1890)

Calthorpe, Lieutenant the Honourable S.J.D., *Letters from Headquarters* (1858)

Cardigan, the Earl of, *Eight Months on Active Service* (1856)

Cardigan versus Calthorpe, lawsuit affidavits (1863)

Carew, Peter, 'One of the Six Hundred (Captain Robert Portal)', *Blackwood's Magazine* (1946); 'Combat and Carnival' (1954)

Cattell, Surgeon William, 'Autobiography of Asst-Surgeon William Cattell (attached 5th Dragoon Guards)' held at the National Army Museum

Cavalry Journal, Captain Lewis Edward Nolan (1911)

Census Returns (1841–1911)

Cleveland, Cornet Archibald, *Letter to his Uncle from Balaclava* (1854)

Clfford VC, Henry, *Letters and Sketches from the Crimea* (1956)

Cornwallis, Major Fiennes, 4th Light Dragoons, *Letters Written from the Crimea* (1868)

Crider, Lawrence W., *In Search of the Light Brigade* (2004)

Cruse, TSM George, *Letters from the Crimea* (1854–55)

Daniell, David S., *4th Hussars: The Story of the 4th Queen's Own Hussars (1685–1958)* (1959)

Doughton, Private Joseph, *Narrative of Joseph Doughton, late of Her Majesty's 13th Light Dragoons, one of the Heroes wounded at the Battle of Balaclava, in the Gallant Cavalry Charge* (1856)

Doyle, Private John, *A Descriptive Account of the Famous Charge of the Light Brigade at Balaclava* (1877)

Duberley, Mrs Henry, *Journal Kept During the Russian War* (1855)

Dutton, Roy, *Forgotten Heroes* (2007)

Ewart, Lt-General J.A., *The Story of a Soldier's Life, Volume 1* (1881)

Farquharson, Pte Robert, *Reminiscences of Crimean Campaigning and Russian Imprisonment* (1883)

Fenton, Roger, *Photographs and Letters from the Crimea* (1954)

Fortesque, the Honourable John, *A History of the 17th Lancers* (1895)

Franks, Sergeant-Major H., *Leaves from a Soldier's Notebook* (1904)

Godman, R. Temple, *The Fields of War* (1977)

Gowing, Timothy, *A Voice from the Ranks* (1884)

Grigg, Sergeant Joseph, account in *Told From the Ranks* (1897)

Herbert, Sergeant James H., 'The Charge of the Light Brigade' *Royal Magazine* (1906)

Hodge, Lieutenant-Colonel Edwin, *Little Hodge* (1971)

Hughes, TSM Edwin, account in the *Blackpool Gazette* (1912)

Hutton, Captain Thomas, letters from the Crimea published in the *4th Hussars Journal* (1933)

Illustrated London News, 'Portraits and Accounts of Eight Survivors' (1875)

Jenyns, Captain Soame, letters published in the *History of the 13th Hussars* (1911)

Kelly, Mrs Tom, *From the Fleet in the Fifties* (1902)

Kinglake, Alexander W., *The Invasion of the Crimea* (9 volumes) (1877–78)

Lamb, Private James, account in the *Strand* Magazine (1891*)*

Lummis, Canon William, *Honour the Light Brigade* (1973)

Mitchell, Sergeant Albert, *Recollections of One of the Light Brigade* (1885)

Mollo, John and Boris, *Uniforms and Equipment of the Light Brigade* (1968)

Morley, RSM Thomas, *The Man of the Hour* (1892)

_____, *The Cause of the Charge of Balaclava* (1899)

Murray, Reverend Robert H., *The History of the 8th King's Royal Irish Hussars* (2 volumes) (1928)

Nolan, Edward Henry, *The Illustrated History of the War against Russia* (2 volumes) (1857)

Nunnerley, Sergeant-Major James, *Short Sketch of the 17th Lancers* (1892)

Paget, Lord George, *The Light Cavalry Brigade in the Crimea* (1881)

Pardoe, Derek, *The Story of One of the Heavy Brigade* (2001)

Parkinson, Sergeant-Major John, 'The Battle of the Alma' *Royal Magazine* (1906)

Parry, D.H., *The Death or Glory Boys* (1899)

Pemberton, W.B., *Battles of the Crimean War* (1962)

Penn, John, account held at the East Lothian Archives

Pennington, Private William, *Left of Six Hundred* (1887)

_____, *Sea, Camp and Stage* (1906)

Portal, Captain C., *Letters from the Crimea* (1900)

Powell, Trumpeter Harry, *Recollections of a Young Soldier during the Crimean War* (1876)

Public Record Office, HQ Records, Crimea (WO 28) Soldiers Discharge Documents: Cavalry of the Line (1855–1872 and 1873–1892)

Richardson, Private John, account in *Spy* magazine (1892)

Ryzhov, Lieutenant-General Ivan Ivanovic, *O Srazhenii pod Balaklave* from *Russkii Vestnik* (1870)

Russell, William H., *The War to the Death of Lord Raglan* (1855)

_____, *The British Expedition to the Crimea* (1877)

_____, *The Great War with Russia* (1895)

Ryan, George, *Our Heroes of the Crimea* (1855)

Seager, Lieutenant Edward, letters from Balaclava published in *The History of the 8th Hussars* (1928)

Smith, RSM George Loy, *A Victorian RSM (including statements by 27 men who were present at Balaclava)* (1987)

Smyth, Ben, letters from Lord Cardigan to A.W. Kinglake in the Kinglake Archive

Sterling, Lieutenant-Colonel Anthony, *The Highland Brigade in the Crimea* (1895)

White-Thompson, Sir Robert, *A Memoir of Lieutenant-Colonel William Morris* (1903)

Whitton, Lieutenant-Colonel Frank, *Deeds Which Should Not Pass Away* (1939)

Wightman, Pte James, 'Balaclava and Russian Captivity' published in *Nineteenth Century* magazine (1892)

Williams, Captain G.T., *Historical Records of the 11th Hussars* (1908)

Wombwell, Captain George, *Letter from Sebastopol* (1854)

Wren, Mr J., late 10th Hussars, letter to the *Daily Telegraph* (1875)

INDEX